OUR GOD IS WONDERFUL

A Companion to *The Wonders of God*

WILLIAM MACDONALD

GOSPEL FOLIO PRESS
P. O. Box 2041, Grand Rapids MI 49501-2041
Available in the UK from
JOHN RITCHIE LTD., Kilmarnock, Scotland

OUR GOD IS WONDERFUL
by William MacDonald
Copyright © 1999
William MacDonald
All rights reserved

Published by Gospel Folio Press
P. O. Box 2041
Grand Rapids, MI 49501-2041

ISBN 1-882701-60-7

Cover design by J. B. Nicholson, Jr.

All Scripture quotations from the New King James Version unless
otherwise noted. New King James Version © 1979, 1980, 1982,
Thomas Nelson, Inc., Publishers.

Printed in the United States of America

CONTENTS

PART I

GOD'S WONDERFUL CREATION

Nature is too thin a screen;
the glory of the omnipresent God
bursts through everywhere.
RALPH WALDO EMERSON

GOD'S WONDERFUL CREATION

O Lord, how great are Your works!
Your thoughts are very deep (Ps. 92:5).

O Lord, how manifold are your works!
In wisdom You have made them all (Ps. 104:24).

He does great things past finding out,
Yes, wonders without number (Job 9:10).

Ah, Lord God! Behold, You have made the
heavens and the earth by Your great power and
outstretched arm. There is nothing too hard
for You (Jer. 32:17).

I have made the earth, and created man on it:
I, even My hands, have stretched out the heavens,
and all their host have I commanded (Isa. 45:12).

"In your journey through life, take time to stop and smell the roses." This advice by golfer Walter Hagen is good but it doesn't go far enough. We should take time to revel in *all*

God's creation. Everything He made is marvelous beyond description. Everyone owes it to himself or herself to be awestruck by the dimensions of the universe, the number of stars, and the precision with which they move. No one should miss the mind-boggling world of potential in the living cell. What a tragedy it would be to go through life hugging the commonplace and missing the beautiful, majoring in the mundane and missing the majestic.

So let's stop and smell the roses and also admire God's works in the universe, the starry heavens, the human body, the brain, animal life, vegetation, and a sampling of God's fingerprints in a few other fields of science. We begin with the universe.

THE UNIVERSE

God existed before the universe. He created it. Although He is wholly apart from it, He is everywhere in it because He is present everywhere at one and the same time.

Its Size

How big is the universe? Actually no one knows. Astronomers are still trying to find the answer to that question. Without telescopic vision, we can see about 2,000 stars. As recently as the 1920s, we thought that our galaxy, the Milky Way, represented the limit of the cosmos. But with the introduction of more powerful telescopes, we realized that it was much more immense than that. Einstein estimated that the circumference of space could be 210,000,000,000,000,000,000,000 light years.

The Hubble Space Telescope has broadened our vision but still does not give us a final answer. With it we can see stars that are billions of light years from the earth. But there's more beyond. At latest count, there are about 50 billion galaxies, each with hundreds of billions of stars, making the star count billions times billions. Even if there were only half that many, it wouldn't make much difference to most of us amateur stargazers. And it wouldn't make much difference to us whether we were using the American definition of billion (a thousand million) or the British billion (a million million). The statistics are so great that they lose their meaning to all but astronomers.

Having said that, we should remember that the multitudinous stars occupy only a small fraction of space. As new and more powerful telescopes orbit in space, the figures change and millions of books become outdated.

When Did the Universe Begin?

How old is the universe? Scientists today estimate that it ranges between 10 and 20 billion years old, and they favor the lower end of the range. How does this square with the biblical view? First of all, it should be clear that Genesis 1:1 is not dated: *"In the beginning, God created the heavens and the earth."* No specific time is mentioned.

Christians who hold to a "young earth" view of cosmology object to a billion-year earth. They would say that God could have created the earth with characteristics of age. He could have created the earth with a built-in appearance of age. He could have created the stars so that they appeared to be millions of light years away. That, of course, is possible. He created Adam as an adult man, not as a baby.

There is room for some disagreement among Christians as to the age of the uninhabited earth. But as for the age of human beings on the earth, that is a different story. The genealogies in the Old Testament do not allow for billions or even millions of years. Even with admitted gaps in the genealogies, man's age on the earth could scarcely be as much as 10,000 years.

Expanding Universe?

Is the universe expanding? It is clear that the heavenly bodies are moving away from us at enormous speed. The marvelous thing is that the planets and stars do not scatter helter-skelter. Although the positions of the stars change with regard to the seasons, they do not change with regard to one another. Because their positions are incredibly predictable, they can be relied on for navigation.

Why So Many Stars?

I have often wondered why God hung so many stars in the sky; I certainly would have been satisfied with many less. Even without telescopic vision, the nighttime display is awesome.

But now, as mentioned above, knowing that there are billions of galaxies, each one harboring billions of stars, we ask ourselves, "Why?"

A first attempt at an answer is that they are a testimony to the greatness of God. They are a tribute to His eternal power and Godhood (Rom 1:20). The Designer is greater than His design. The Creator is greater than His creation. If He can sparkle space with so many celestial bodies and call them all by name (Ps. 147:4), He must be great beyond description.

In reading the book of Revelation, the 24 elders say:

Thou art worthy, O Lord, to receive glory and honor and power: for Thou hast created all things, and for Thy pleasure they are and were created (4:11, KJV).

So that is another reason for the multitudinous stars. They were created for God's pleasure. It makes sense. When He made them on the fourth day, is it any wonder that He saw that everything was good? Why should He not be pleased with His handiwork in the stellar heavens?

Now we come across another reason. This time it is not from the Bible, but from physics and astronomy. Physicists today tell us that the approximately 100 billion trillion stars in the heavens, no more and no fewer, are necessary for life on earth to be possible. "Evidently God cared so much for living creatures that he constructed 100 billion trillion stars and carefully crafted them throughout the age of the universe so that at this brief moment in the history of the cosmos humans could exist and have a pleasant place to live."[1]

No wonder that a non-believing scientist has acknowledged that a super intellect has monkeyed with physics.[2] Another one said that "the laws of [physics] seem themselves to be the product of exceedingly ingenious design. The impression of design is overwhelming."[3] Astrophysicist George Greenstein of Amherst College concluded, "As we survey all the evidence, the thought insistently arises that some supernatural agency—or, rather, Agency—must be involved. Is it possible that suddenly, without intending to, we have stumbled upon scientific proof of the existence of a Supreme Being? Was it God who stepped in and so providentially crafted the cosmos for our benefit?"[4]

I am satisfied. The stars are just the right number, no more and no less.

History in the Skies

Where are the stars now? A fascinating thing about the stars is that we do not see them where they are now. We see them as they were when the light that now enters our telescopes left them. So the stars are history rather than current events.

As to the number of the stars, Sir James Jeans, the English physicist, astronomer, and author wrote:

A few stars are known, which are hardly bigger than the earth, but the majority are so large that hundreds of thousands of earths could be packed inside each and have room to spare; here and there we come upon a giant star large enough to contain millions and millions of earths. The total number of stars in the universe is probably something like the total number of grains of sands on all the shores of the world. Such is the littleness of our home in space, when measured up against the total substance of the universe.[5]

We should be filled with a sense of wonder.

The Sun

At the core of the sun, nuclear fusion occurs, explosively discharging gamma radiation that is equal to 100 billion one-megaton hydrogen bombs per second.

The amount of energy that the sun contributes to the earth is approximately 15,000 times the current annual energy consumption of the world's population. The earth receives 10 times as much solar energy every year as that which exists in fossil reserves (coal, oil, *etc.*) and uranium deposits combined. Yet only a two-billionth part of the sun's energy affects the earth.

The sun is the size of 1,300,000 earths. But compared to the star Antarus it is not so huge. If Antarus were hollow, it could hold 64 million suns. Epsilon, the largest known star, could hold 27 billion suns. Our minds cannot comprehend that.

A single day without the sun would mean oblivion for life on earth.

At its present rate, the sun would burn itself out in five billion years.

As we contemplate the heavenly bodies, we have to agree with poet Joseph Addison:

> *In Reason's ear they all rejoice,*
> *And utter forth a glorious Voice,*

Forever singing as they shine,
"The Hand that made us is divine."

PLANET EARTH

He has made the earth by His power, He has established
the world by His wisdom, and has stretched out the
heavens at His discretion (Jer. 10:12).

"Earth itself is a masterpiece, a well-tuned organism whirling through space. From hidden underwater worlds burgeoning with exotic life forms to the destructive power of an erupting volcano, nature is never less than impressive."[6]

Earth is a mote of dust in the universe, and as someone has said "Man is a speck on a speck, called Earth, controlled by a speck—the sun—in a speck, our galaxy."

Stephen Hawking has described the earth as "a medium-sized planet orbiting around an average star in the outer suburbs of an ordinary spiral galaxy, which is itself only one of about a million million galaxies in the observable universe."[7]

The whirling sphere on which we live is a masterpiece of creativity. As it spins through space, its direction is well regulated and predictable. In spite of its ceaseless motion, we can live on it comfortably without any sign of dizziness.

The earth spins at approximately 1040 miles per hour at the equator. It moves around the sun at an average of 18.5 miles per second. The sun moves around the Milky Way at 150-155 miles per second. Our Milky Way moves within a cluster of galaxies at about 75 miles per second. Like it or not, we are in the fast lane of the universe.

Planet earth is a masterpiece of beauty, whether we gaze at purple mountain majesties or snow-capped heights.

There are the oceans white with foam, ceaselessly pounding the shores and shaping photogenic sand dunes. Or the placid lakes beckoning us to come with our lines, hooks, and bait. Newlyweds stand silently, watching Niagara's awesome plunge. Tourists laden with cameras, tripods, and film try in vain to capture a full view of the Grand Canyon, earth's deepest scar. The landscape is decked with flowers that exceed the beauty of Solomon's royal apparel, and stands of forest give earth the name Green Planet. We must not forget the coral reefs, teeming with living organisms, the unique beauty of the painted deserts, or conversation-stopping rainbows. The four seasons provide variety. As day dies in the west, the crimson horizon shines through swatches of clouds.

God must love beauty; He made so much of it.

Our Ideal Environment

It's marvelous how well suited Planet Earth is for sustaining life. As far as we know, it is the only planet that has that distinction. Take for instance, the air we breathe. It has just the right combination of nitrogen, oxygen, argon, and carbon dioxide. Man breathes out carbon dioxide, which is poisonous. Plants breathe out oxygen. The plants live on the carbon dioxide whereas man needs oxygen.

The distance of the earth from the sun guards us from roasting or freezing. A 2% change in average yearly temperature would be disastrous.

The speed of the earth around the sun is optimum in keeping it from getting too close to the heat or straying too far from it.

Do you enjoy the four seasons? Well, that's because the earth's axis of rotation is adjusted to the proper tilt of 23° instead of being at a 90° or some other angle.

The speed of the earth's rotation on its axis results in a

24-hour day, which couldn't be better planned for living forms.

If the moon were much nearer the earth, enormous tides would inundate most or all of it. Recent studies show that it's the moon that maintains the earth's life-sustaining tilt.

The right proportion of land and water covers the planet. The 70% of water stabilizes both the temperature swings of day and night and the temperature of the surface of the oceans, then provides the right amount of rainfall. Yet if the mountains were leveled, our planet would be covered by water. Incidentally, our planet is the only one in the solar system that is thought to have water in liquid form. What a "coincidence."

Like most substances, water contracts when it is cooled, but unlike every other substance, this contraction stops at 4 degrees Centigrade. Then water does an about face and expands until it freezes. The result is that the bonds between molecules in the ice are less tightly knit. In other words, ice is less dense than water and so it floats rather than sinking to the bottom of oceans and lakes. The top layer of ice in a pond helps to maintain the warmer temperature of water below. If ice sank, oceans and lakes would freeze solid, killing fish and water plants. We have to appreciate the creative Intelligence that causes liquid water and ice to behave in this unique way. If air acted like this on earth's surface, the temperature would be too hot for humans, animals, and vegetation to survive.

Gravity is the proper strength. If it had been stronger, stars would have burned much faster and hotter and the sun would long since have used up its hydrogen. If gravity were weaker, all stars would be dim "red dwarfs."

Because conditions on earth are so finely tuned, we have winds that keep plants and other forms of life from baking. Winds carry away pollution, and deliver oxygen where it is needed. We have water, the universal solvent, without which there would be no living thing. The sun warms the ocean, causing water to evaporate, rise into the sky, condense in drops that form on particles of dust to form clouds. The clouds carry the water across the face of the earth, then drop it as rain, snow, and hail.

Because the density of the atmosphere is right, most meteors burn up before they get to the earth.

Most of the surface of the dry land is covered with topsoil, teeming with life and seeds, and producing vegetation.

Ocean currents keep most of the water in liquid form.

In his book, *Earth, the Place for Life*, astrophysicist Hugh Ross lists 33 ways in which Planet Earth has been created and positioned in order to support human life.

"Finely tuned" is an apt description of creation. Only an Intelligent Mind could have done it. To think that it is random and undirected without plan or purpose stretches credulity.

An article titled "That Astounding Creator—Nature" appeared in *Our Amazing World of Nature*, a Reader's Digest publication. It is sheer folly to attribute to "nature" the power and wisdom that only God possesses.

THE HUMAN BODY

The human body begins when sperm and egg combine to make a single living cell. This cell contains a coil of building blocks known as DNA, carrying a code that determines what the person-to-be will be like.

The original cell multiplies until billions of cells make a body. But don't think of these cells as inert blobs of gelatin. Every one of them is a living entity with vast possibilities. Each cell knows what its function is and to what part of the body it belongs. Although it is microscopically small, it houses activities comparable to those of a modern city.

Few writers can rhapsodize over the wonders of the cell better than Lewis Thomas. Speaking of the marvel of a single cell growing into a human brain, he wrote:

The mere existence of that cell should be one of the greatest astonishments of the earth. People ought to be walking around all day, all through their waking hours, calling to others in endless wonderment, talking of nothing except that cell. It is an unbelievable thing, and yet there it is, popping neatly into its place amid the jumbled cells of every one of the several billion human embryos around the planet, just as if it were the easiest thing in the world to do.

One cell is switched on to become the whole trillion-cell, massive apparatus for thinking and imagining and, for that matter, being surprised. All the information needed for learning to read and write, playing the piano, arguing before senatorial subcommittees, walking across a street through traffic, or the marvelous act of putting out one hand and leaning against a tree, is contained in that first cell. All of grammar, all syntax, all arithmetic, all music.

No one has a ghost of an idea how this works, and nothing else in life can be so puzzling. If anyone does succeed in explaining it, within my lifetime, I will charter a skywriting airplane, maybe a whole fleet of them, and send them aloft to write one great exclamation point after another, around the whole sky, until all my money runs out.[8]

Writing in *Our Amazing World of Nature*, science writer Rutherford Platt says:

The nucleus of each cell holds a rolled-up coil of DNA's exquisite tapelike molecules that carry the code of life on them the way a magnetic tape carries music.

When future generations look back to our space age, they

may well regard the exploration of inner space—the depths of the living cell—as far more important to humanity than the spectacular achievements of the astronauts.[9]

In *The Incredible Machine*, published by the National Geographic Society, we find a similar outburst of amazement:

The events...that take life all the way from a solitary primordial cell to the convolutions of the human brain and the self-consciousness of the human mind should be sweeping us off our feet in amazement.[10]

The Brain

The brain is "the most complex object in the known universe." Drs. Don DeYoung and Richard Bliss write:

Our brain remains a frontier of science; we actually know very little about it, but what is known is overwhelming. In addition, every single neuronal cell within the brain contains a trillion atoms. This is like a microscopic universe within each cell, complete with order, purpose, and interdependence of components.[11]

An article in *Time* magazine admitted that the way in which "the million cells of the human brain work together to create consciousness is the master unsolved problem of biology."[12]

The human mind theorizes, philosophizes, rationalizes, judgmentalizes, moralizes, theologizes. It draws conclusions, forms convictions, invents ideas, and differentiates between truth and error, good and evil. It remembers, compares, and contrasts.[13]

It contains imagination, morality, sensuality, mathematics,

memory, humor, judgment, religion, as well as an incredible catalog of facts and theories and the common sense to assign them all priority and significance.[14]

The coordination of mind and muscle is a marvel. Take the case of a church organist I know. There are five keyboards on his organ, with 61 keys on each one—a total of 301 keys. In addition, there are 150 stops and 32 pedals. As he reads the notes, the brain sends direction to his hands and feet to play the keys and pedals simultaneously and to pull the stops whenever necessary. As a result the church building is filled with exquisite harmony. Of course, he has to practice for hours to train his fingers and feet, but his mind never shifts into neutral. He must constantly think of the next chord and how to produce it.

The brain has the distinction of being the only part of the body that is not replaced every 7 years.

Roscoe Drummond, in a whimsical mood, said, "The mind is a wonderful thing. It starts working the minute you're born and never stops until you get up to speak in public."

It tortures common sense to think that the brain happened without Intelligent Design.

The Growth of the Body

As the cells multiply, some produce proteins that in turn make blood to supply oxygen and insulin to control energy, and collagen to build skin. Soon nerves, veins, and organs form in the proper places and in the right sequence. Programmed in that single cell are heart, lungs, gall bladder, kidneys, cartilage, pancreas, eyes, ears, skin, skeletal structure, nerves, brains, and everything else necessary for a normal body. We can describe what happens but we don't know how or why.

Often expectant women have quirky hungers. It seems strange to want pizza and ice cream at the same time. But those foods have chemicals that the body needs. So it sends a wish list to the brain and the brain in turn goes to work on the appetite.

Just before a baby is born, the placenta takes some of the mother's gamma globulin and transfers it to the unborn's bloodstream. This plasma or serum contains antibodies to fight diseases that had previously infected the mother. This spares babies from contracting any of those diseases until they can manufacture their own antibodies.

A Baby is Born

In about nine months the baby is well formed and makes his or her debut to its doting family. Infants are born without teeth, a kindly arrangement for mothers who nurse them. The baby's jaws are constructed with tremendous powers of suction, a feature that is lost as the child grows older. Just try to drink milk through a rubber nipple.

All the nutrients necessary for good health are present and in the proper balance in a mother's milk. The early milk, called colostrum, contains cells that attack bacteria and are able to produce antibodies that destroy viruses.

That little human body has its own air conditioning system, its waste management, a communication center, a power station, a water pumping system, and an infection battling hospital. There is a photographic studio in the eye-brain system, a concert hall with vocal chords and auditory system, and a 24-hour-a-day chemical laboratory conducted in every cell of the body.

The baby has every sensory faculty that it ever will have: taste, touch, sight, hearing, smell. From then on it's just a matter of developing them.

A person could spend a lifetime becoming acquainted

with any of the body's parts. That is why we have doctors who are "specialists": cardiologists, neurologists, ophthalmologists, rheumatologists, and so forth.

Members of the Body

To think of just a few body parts reveals how amazing they are.

(a) *Blood:* Five or six quarts of blood are constantly flowing through 60,000 miles of blood vessels to ferry oxygen from the lungs to the 200 trillion cells of the body. But oxygen is not all the blood supplies. It services the cells with sodium, potassium, calcium, magnesium, amino acids, sugars, nitrogen, and a lot of other things we didn't even know we needed.

Further, the blood has a clever way of gathering impurities, toxins, and undesirable chemicals and gases, and shunting them to organs that will eliminate them from the body. The kidneys excel in doing this. They are phenomenal filters.

A drop of blood contains millions of red cells and thousands of white cells and platelets. When we cut ourselves, the platelets rush to the scene and spin a web on which red cells cluster; then the blood clots and the bleeding stops.

A red cell moves with impressive speed and efficiency for four months. Then it drifts off to the spleen where it is recycled.

When harmful bacteria invade the body, the white cells declare war. Some use chemical warfare and some use heavier ammunition. If there aren't enough white cells, bone marrow sends added reserves and antibodies guide them to their intended target. White cells are designed for specific targets. An anti-chicken pox cell won't do for scarlet fever. Once a lymph node produces an antibody, it keeps a record of the formula for ready reference in the future because it takes time for the body to decipher the code of an invader.

(b) *Bones:* Once I broke the fifth metatarsal in my right foot. All the doctor did was wind gauze around it; he called it a wet cast. He assured me that it would heal itself and it did. A cartilage forms around the break, holding the two pieces of bone together.

It is not by chance that the joints of the human body have a lubricating system. Synovial fluid makes it possible for bones to carry the weight of the body while moving easily and smoothly against one another at the joints. Think what it would be like if walking and running produced a cacophony of screeches and squeaks.

(c) *The Hand:* Someone has called the hand "a bewildering array of levers, hinges, and power sources, all managed by the master computer, the brain."

(d) *The Thumb:* We take for granted that we have an opposable thumb, that is, that we can touch all four fingers of the hand with our thumb. It is this that makes the hand the greatest tool and the most versatile instrument in the world. Picture how limited you would be if you lost a thumb. You would have difficulty opening a can, turning a knob, or playing a piano. With it you can do a thousand tasks that otherwise would be out of the question. The thumb is the doctor's most useful instrument to stop bleeding.

(e) *Ears:* We hear when sound vibrations hit the eardrum. Missionary doctor Paul Brand explains:

> Ordinary conversation causes air molecules to vibrate and move the eardrum a mere ten-thousandth of a centimeter, but with enough precision to differentiate all the sounds of human speech. The eardrum membrane has the flexibility to register the drop of a straight pin as well as the noise of a New York

subway one hundred trillion times louder. It could hardly be more sensitive; if ear sensitivity increased by a tiny amount, we would hear the movement of air molecules as a constant whishing sound (this affliction actually plagues some people, with disastrous hallucinatory effects).

Survivors of high school biology should know what happens after the eardrum vibrates: three tiny bones, informally known as the hammer, anvil, and stirrup, transfer that vibration into the middle ear. I have worked with most of the bones in the human body, and none are more remarkable than these three, the body's smallest. Unlike every other bone, these do not grow with age—a one-day old infant has them fully developed. They are in constant, unrelieved motion, since every sound that reaches us causes these bones to swing into action. Working together, they magnify the forces that vibrate the eardrum until it is twenty times greater than when it entered.[15]

The number of vibrations per second is what determines a particular pitch.

(f) *The Nose:* Don't take your nose for granted. It is a marvel. It senses fragrances, and the brain records them. That is why we can relive a Chinese meal in a Hong Kong hotel, or recognize the fragrance of an orange grove in Israel after 40 years.

Taste buds live only three or four days but the taste is coded in the brain.

(g) *The Feet:* If you live to be 70, your feet will have taken you around the earth three times. Isn't that enough to make you feel tired?

You never realize how important a toe can be until it is injured or amputated. When a Hall of Fame baseball player broke a toe, he noticed that it affected his delivery and indirectly strained his arm. His skill was never the same.

(h) *Memory:* Did you ever wonder what life would be

like if we didn't have the power of remembering? F. B. Meyer tackled the question and came up with this:

> Memory is one of the most wonderful processes of our nature. It is the faculty that enables us to record and recall the past. If it were not for this power the mind would remain forever in the blank condition of childhood, and all that had ever passed before it would leave no more impression than images do upon the plain surface of a mirror...The one fact of interest to us is that it has a universal retentiveness. Nothing has ever passed across it that has not left a record on its plastic slabs.[16]

There is one merciful exception in the area of memory. Pain is quickly forgotten. We can remember that we had it, but we can't recall the pain itself. Jesus pointed this out in a graphic manner:

> *A woman, when she is in labor, has sorrow because her hour has come; but as soon as she has given birth to the child, she no longer remember the anguish, for joy that a human being has been born into the world* (Jn. 16:21).

(i) *The Digestive Apparatus:* The digestive system is a vast complex apparatus that carries on its work with astounding precision and well-timed interaction. It is beyond the scope of this book to describe it in great detail. The following sketch reveals only a sample of what is involved.

Much of our bodies consist of protein, and the food we eat contains protein. But how can the body digest these food proteins without at the same time digesting itself? It's quite a marvel.

When we eat proteins like meat and cheese, the stomach stimulates the production of a hormone called gastrin, which in turn stimulates the secretion of hydrochloric acid.

(That's the burning fluid that comes back into your throat when you eat too much pizza before going to bed.) The acid acts as an antiseptic and kills most bacteria and foreign cells. It also breaks down proteins to aid in their digestion.

As the partially digested food moves down into the small intestine, the high acid level triggers the flow of a hormone called secretin into the blood. Secretin tells the pancreas to produce bicarbonate, the same soda that we have in our pantry. This protects the small intestine by neutralizing the acid.

As partially digested proteins enter the small intestine, a hormone with an unpronounceable name produces three different enzymes. As long as these enzymes are in the pancreas, they can't dissolve the proteins of which that organ is made. They are inhibited by a small component which acts like a switch.

But when they move down into the small intestine with the partially digested food, an enzyme that is produced only in this intestine removes the microscopic component, thus activating the enzymes. They then digest the food proteins but protect the small intestine from digesting itself.

This marvelous sequence of actions is only a fraction of those that take place when we eat. And they could not have developed over millions of years. All of them had to be together from the beginning for the digestive tract to function properly.

(j) *The Liver:* The liver is an amazing machine that produces 1,000 different enzymes. Among other accomplishments, these enzymes keep the blood pure. If the surgeon cuts away some of the liver, it will grow back to size in a few months.

Lewis Thomas has some delightful thoughts about the liver. If he were told to take control of his liver and perform its functions, he said he would rather be put in charge of a 747 jet from his coach seat.

> I am, to face the facts squarely, considerably less intelligent than my liver. I am, moreover, constitutionally unable to make hepatic decisions, and I prefer not to be obliged to, ever. I would not be able to think of the first thing to do. [17]

(k) *Unconscious Reflexes:* Some of our bodily functions take place automatically. The heart beats and the blood flows without any effort on our part. The digestive system carries on its important work without any conscious help from us. We don't have to control our kidneys, liver, or pancreas. They know what to do, and do it.

Ordinarily we breathe instinctively, but we can also do it by our own will when the doctor puts his stethoscope to our chest and tells us to inhale and exhale. The urge to breathe continually, awake and asleep, is so strong that we can't end our life by holding our breath.

We can blink when we want to, but most of our blinking is spontaneous. We do it 20,000 times a day. If we had to initiate each blink, we would never get any work done. So God has devised this mechanism to make sure that the surface of our eyes stays moist.

(l) *Miscellaneous Wonders:* Why don't two parents, in separate fertilizations, produce identical babies? There are so many possible combinations of DNA that the odds against this happening are about 70 trillion to one. In other words the chance is infinitesimal.[18]

You have probably read about women who seem unable to bear children. In their desperation, they adopt a child. Soon afterward, they become pregnant. Why?

One time a dentist had a hard time extracting one of my teeth. The reluctant molar splintered in his forceps. Months later, as I ran my tongue over the toothless gum, I felt a sharp prick. In time, a shard of tooth emerged. How did the splinter know to come out there and not travel to my heart and puncture it?

What would it cost to make a human body? Biophysicist Harold J. Morowitz of Yale University said that to fashion the proteins, enzymes, RNA, DNA, amino acids, and other complex biochemicals that make up the stuff of life "might cost six quadrillion dollars. Assembling the resulting heap of cells into tissue, the tissue into organs, and the organs into a warm body might drain all the treasures of the world, with no guarantee of success"[19] And even that many dollars could not produce consciousness or a spirit within the body.

The tissues of a pig are more compatible with human tissues than those of a chimpanzee. The human body rejects them least. Many people are living normal lives with an aortic valve made of pig skin. Even the liver of a pig has been transplanted to a human.

How can the brain think what middle C on the piano sounds like, then control the vocal chords to produce that exact sound?

There is a tiny, insignificant worm with the elegant name *C. elegans*. It is so small that you probably wouldn't see it if you weren't looking for it. Yet the genetic information coded on its 97 million base pairs of DNA would fill more volumes than a complete set of *Encyclopedia Britannica.*

The body has marvelous powers to heal itself. That is why the doctor says, "Take two aspirins and call me in the morning." Most things are better by the morning.

THE HUMAN SPIRIT

Man is a tripartite being consisting of spirit, soul, and body. The spirit is what enables us to have fellowship with

God. The soul is the seat of our emotions. The body is the structure in which our spirit and soul dwell.

The body is not the person. We can live without the body. When believers die, their body goes to the grave, but their spirit and soul enjoy conscious existence in heaven. God the Father does not have a body: He is spirit. Before the incarnation, Jesus did not have a body, yet He was a living Person with intellect, emotions, and will.

The Bible always mentions the spirit first, because it is the most important. People invariably mention the body first (body, soul, and spirit) because it is the part they can see.

The spirit has intelligence apart from the brain. Dying, comatose Christians rarely respond to ordinary subjects of conversation, yet they indicate recognition when a Scripture is read or a prayer is offered. Believers with Alzheimer's disease may be removed from reality, yet often they will mouth the words of a hymn when it is sung in their presence.

The account of the rich man and Lazarus (Lk. 16:19-31) confirms that there is intelligence beyond that of the brain. Both men died. Their bodies, including their brains, decayed and eventually returned to dust. The rich man went to hades, whereas Lazarus found himself in Abraham's bosom, a poetic name for heaven. The rich man could speak, see, suffer, recognize Abraham, reason, and plead for his brothers. Lazarus presumably had the same faculties.

There is no such thing in the Bible as "soul sleep." Paul describes the body as sleeping but never the soul or spirit. To be absent from the body is to be present with the Lord (2 Cor. 5:6-9). This is far better.

The spirit, soul, and body are closely related. What affects one affects the other. The *British Medical Journal* once reported that there is not a single cell in the body that is totally removed from the spirit.

A hospital patient had recovered favorably from a fractured hip, and the doctor told her daughter that she could take her mother home the next day. The daughter had other plans. She and her husband had decided to put her mother in an old folks home. The mother was devastated. When an intern checked her a few hours later, she was showing general physical deterioration. Within 24 hours she died—not of a broken hip but of a broken heart.

ALL CREATURES GREAT AND SMALL

But now ask the beasts, and they will teach you; and the birds of the air, and they will tell you; or speak to the earth, and it will teach you; and the fish of the sea will explain to you.
Who among all these does not know that the hand of the Lord has done this, in whose hand is the life of every living thing, and the breath of all mankind? (Job 12:7-10)

Mammals

Farmers see the hand of God when they watch a sow giving birth to little ones. The mother lies on her side, ready for the moment when her offspring arrive. The first piglet appears and immediately begins its wiggling crawl. It could go north, east, or any direction between. But it doesn't. It moves south, drags itself around the sow's rear legs, and makes straight for the feeding station. One after another, the newborn follow the same route. How do they know?

The idea that a giraffe has an elongated neck because it reached for leaves in the trees in order to survive is nonsense. The reason its neck is long is because God created it that way. If it depended on evolution's millions of years, it would have become extinct in the meantime.

The camel was made for desert life. The dromedary, for instance, can live off the fat in its hump when food is scarce. It can travel eight days without water. Its wide hooves have a tough piece of skin between the toes, which prevents its feet from sinking into the sand. Special muscles in its nostrils close part way, keeping the sand out and letting air in. Long eyelashes protect its eyes from blowing sand. If a grain of sand should slip through, an inner eyelid wipes it off.

The pocket gopher, about the size of a hamster, lives underground most of the time. Claws that grow 20 inches per year enable it to build a network of passages. Near its eyes is a gland that produces a sort of jelly the purpose of which is to snag dirt so it won't go into the gopher's eyes. This little fellow's lips are behind its big buckteeth; they keep out the dirt when it chews on a tasty carrot morsel. If a farmer sees a carrot plant suddenly disappear into the ground, he might suspect that one of these little rodents is at work.

Because of a dog's acute sense of smell, a Labrador named Snag helped the U.S. Customs service make 118 drug seizures worth $810 million.

The bat is a nocturnal flying mammal with eyes that can spot a sleeping insect and ears that can hear a caterpillar munching leaves. Only on the darkest nights does it turn on its sonar: it emits 50,000 to 100,000 echo-location signals per second through its nose, then hears sound waves that bounce off its doomed prey.[20]

What animal kills more people than any other except snakes or bees? If you said scorpions, you would be right. Only a small percent of them are lethal, but the poison of some deadly varieties is 100,000 times more powerful than cyanide. For most people they are a "nightmare incarnate." They have been called "the least favorite organisms on

Earth" (unless, of course, you happen to be a 10-year-old boy who is fascinated by them and edges ever nearer so that he can get a closer view while his mother goes into emotional orbit). If you live under a thatched roof, you might watch them crawling on the thatch over your bed. This possibility is not calculated to ensure a good night's rest.[21]

The blue whale is not only the largest animal; it is the loudest. Its low frequency pulses can be detected 530 miles away.

The phrase "a gentle alligator" sounds like an oxymoron. But in spite of its 70-odd teeth, a female is gentle with its dozen or so eggs.

> As the embryos incubate in the sun, they emit carbon dioxide, which seeps into the nest, forming a weak acid that coats the eggs. Slowly the shell thins. Gently grasping an egg in her mouth, she rolls it on her tongue, feeling for signs of life. After nine weeks, some hatchlings can poke their snouts through the shell and emerge, while others emit grunts that elicit help from the mother.[22]

Dolly was the first sheep to be cloned. She is a reasonable facsimile of her mother. However, there's a problem. She inherits her mother's genetic code which determines physical characteristics and thousands of vital biological processes of living—and of dying. The mature animal that has been used for cloning has a biological "life clock" that has already run down part way. The clone appears to inherit that "life clock." It does not come into existence as a newborn baby would, but as a creature whose years are already partly spent.

Birds

In a state park in California, I spotted this sign: "The

small world of a big tree. Thick, fibrous Sequoia bark insulates the tree from periodic fires. Chipmunks and robins take dust baths in powdered bark, using its tannin as a flea repellent." Who would think that these little creatures would discover the insecticide property of the powdered bark of a redwood tree?

There is cooperation in the woods. A wildlife expert saw a young blue jay bring food to an adult jay, "a grizzled veteran, whose bill was broken."

When the blackpoll warbler feels autumn's frost, it devours great gobs of yellow fat to nourish it on its long flight south. It pigs out so much that it can scarcely take off, but once in flight it can continue nonstop from New England to South America, a distance of 2,000 miles. It knows how to avoid storms, and sometimes climbs to 16,000 feet to get a boost from favorable winds. Somehow it can survive with little oxygen at altitudes where you and I couldn't.

A Ruppell's vulture can fly at 37,000 feet. One collided with a plane at that altitude. The plane was able to land safely, but the vulture didn't.[23]

Guillemots live on rocky cliffs in the Arctic. They overpopulate a region so much that females lay their eggs side by side in a long row on a narrow ledge. There are hundreds of eggs, yet the females know their own. If you move one to a new location, the mother will find it and return it to its proper place. How does she know?[24]

A young sooty tern never lands for three to ten years before finally returning to earth to breed. It eats, drinks, and sleeps in flight. Each spring the arctic tern travels 11,000 miles over the sea to its nesting place.

Some genetic secret in a female blue tit determines the sex of her offspring. If the male is healthy and strong, she will produce more sons. If the male is not so robust, there will be fewer male chicks.[25]

The woodpecker finch, native to the Galapagos Islands, uses a cactus needle as a tool to spear grubs out of their holes in the trees. If the trees could talk, they would thank the birds for ridding them of these pests. In the meantime, the finches would go on happily munching the grubs. Crows in New Caledonia are also toolmakers. Like the woodpecker, they make a spear to drag prey out of holes. They are the only non-human creatures known to make a tool with a hook at the end of it.[26]

White-collar swifts build their nests behind waterfalls for protection. They don't mind flying through the falls to get home. Due to their long and narrow wing designs, they can fly at 70 miles per hour at an altitude of over one mile.

The Old World palm swift builds its nest on the backside of a palm frond that grows downward. It plucks some of its own feathers, then with a glue-like saliva, sticks the feathers to the frond. After laying an egg on a horizontal surface, the swift carries it to its nest and secures it there with more sticky saliva. When it sits on the eggs, it covers them with the part of its breast where the feathers are missing. The bare skin is warmer.

The palm swift detects when there is bad weather ahead by changes in the barometric pressure. So it changes direction, flying at a right angle to its original direction and thus skirts around the storm.

When the insect population is low, the finch hooks its claws to a tree or barn and becomes torpid. Its heart beats more slowly and its breathing almost stops. Thus the bird is highly energy efficient until swarms of insects appear again.

Wild birds cannot lay eggs if there is no mate. Domestic birds can. One hen laid 1,515 eggs in eight years without ever seeing a rooster.[27]

A hen can take gravel into its gullet and melt it down to produce eggshells. Why doesn't acid of that strength destroy the hen's insides? Every time I make an omelet, I am glad that the Lord made the shell as He did. Suppose it were like bone china. It would splinter in a thousand pieces and make my breakfast a grating, scratching irritation instead of a gastronomic delight. As you know, God designed the eggshell to be lined with an inner membrane that keeps the broken bits from falling into the bowl. Auto manufacturers copycatted this in making windshields. There is a membrane between layers of glass that binds the shards of a broken windshield so that it falls out as one tangled mass.

The quills of a bird's feather are hollow. This means less weight to carry. If a feather falls out of one wing, the corresponding feather in the other wing will fall out, thus ensuring evenness of flight.

Does a woodpecker get headaches? If it does, it would be understandable. The force with which its head drives its beak against a tree and then stops suddenly should be enough to scramble its brains, especially when the forward movement is stopped in a split second. But scramble them it does not. The woodpecker's skull is constructed to absorb the shock and its bill is of such high strength that it can penetrate bark and wood without being bent or shattered. This bird combines features of a machine gun and a jackhammer.

But why does it endure such banging in order to make holes in a tree? These holes make ideal pantries to store acorns and traps for bark beetles, a gourmet treat for a hungry woodpecker. To retrieve these tasty morsels, the bird has a long, sticky tongue. When not in use, this tongue can be retracted into the head, like the wheels of a jetliner.

A woodpecker had to have all these features from the

time of the first such bird. If they had been added gradually over many years, our rat-a-tat friend would not have survived.

Somehow a barnyard hen senses that she is going to have a family, so she gathers straws and sticks to make a nest (unless the farmer has already provided one). Then she begins to lay a clutch of fertilized eggs.

The eggs must be kept warm, so the hen patiently sits on them. Of course, she must leave from time to time for food and water, but she knows not to overstay her absence from the nest. Otherwise the eggs would get too cold and the incubation would stop.

From time to time the eggs must be turned around. The mother hen deftly takes care of this procedure without benefit of hands.

It takes about 21 days for the chick to form in the egg. Then comes the problem of how to get out of it. No problem. The baby chick is equipped with a cover on its beak, hard enough to break through the shell. As soon as that happens, the stiff cover is discarded. It is no longer needed.

The mother hen keeps careful watch on her little ones until they are safe and able to fend for themselves. For centuries this reproductive ceremony has been going on, each step a marvel of Intelligent Design.

Every morning Farmer Brown went out to his hen house to collect the eggs, he noticed that one or two hens were missing. His efforts to find the predator were futile until someone mentioned that some minks had been seen in the neighborhood. He tried unsuccessfully to trap them. Then a neighbor advised him to add a couple of geese to the flock. That solved the problem. The minks had a healthy respect for geese, and stayed as far away as possible.

A wading bird called the phalarope has a problem. It likes to feed on shrimp, but sometimes those tasty morsels are too far down for this shorebird to reach. The wading bird has a novel way of solving the dilemma. It starts to spin in the water like a top or a whirling dervish. Rotating its body at one complete spin per second, it creates a vortex that sucks up shrimp from a depth of three feet.

A UCLA biologist, William N. Hamner, says that "phalaropes detect prey, thrust, seize, transport, and swallow in less than half a second, at a rate of 180 pecks per minute."[28]

Thanks to the phalarope's ingenuity, it enjoys home delivery.

One ear of an owl points forward, the other backward. This gives it the ability to detect where a sound comes from. Its hearing is so accurate that if blindfolded, it could locate a mouse running across hay in a barn.

Fish

The lungfish breathes air. Unless it surfaces every 20 minutes, it will drown. When the water holes of Africa begin to dry up, the fish wraps itself in mud and waits for the rain, sometimes for years.

The triggerfish has a sharp needle spine that lies flat when there is no danger. But when a predator appears, the spine is hinged to become erect. Another hinge maintains it in that upright position. Any fish that tries to swallow it is in danger of ripping its throat. The spine serves another purpose. It secures the fish in its cave at night, so it can sleep without fear of being swept out to sea by the tide.

The goby fish of Japan is a gender-bender. Its size determines whether it remains a female, becomes a male, or switches back and forth. In a tank with several gobys, the largest will become a male. But put that male in a tank with a larger male and it will switch back to become a female. Other fish change gender, but the goby is the only one that can change back and forth.[29]

Certain shrimps in the Bahamas attract fish, then mount on them and clean their surfaces. Fish line up to be served, just as we would at a car wash. Without these shrimps, the fish would develop ulcers.

Reptiles

An all-female species of lizard in the West Indies and South America reproduces without male contact. There are no males. The unfertilized eggs produce females generation after generation.

Komodo dragons, the largest lizards, can grow to nine feet or more in length and can weigh up to 200 pounds. They have yellow forked tongues that shoot out like flames. They eat poisonous snakes, birds, small mammals, deer, pigs, water buffaloes, and have been known to kill humans. They explode the contention that all dragons are mythical beasts.[30]

The saliva of a Komodo, containing over 50 different kinds of bacteria, is extremely poisonous. The infection that follows a bite kills an animal in about 72 hours. When a dragon chews on a carcass, it often bites its own gums, sending the bacteria into the bloodstream. But its life is not imperiled. There is a protein molecule in the blood that kills the bacteria in the saliva. Chemists are trying to make a synthetic protein molecule or peptide that will become a super-antibiotic.

When you are in India, be careful to avoid "the eleven-step adder." The venom is so deadly that when bitten you can take only 11 steps before keeling over in death. If the venom enters a major vein, it causes the blood to clot and cut off circulation. If it enters a minor blood vessel, however, it makes it impossible for the blood to clot. The same poison can have opposite results.

Insects

Leaf-cutter ants are remarkable little farmers, a greater marvel than researchers had known until recently. Larger members of the complex social community busily range through the forest and cut off leaves that they can carry back to the farm. According to estimates, over time these ants bring 15% of tropical forest vegetation into their chambers.

Now it is time for a smaller species of these ants to shred and pulverize the leafy material, then mix it with their own waste. This becomes food for a mushroom-like fungus, which, in turn, is the food of the ants. But what about the poisons that many of the leaves contain? The fungus is able to break down these toxic materials and then feed on them.

Still smaller ants harvest the fungus when it is full-grown.

In any farming operation, there is always the danger of insects and molds. That is true here. Foreign insects entering the farm carry a parasitic mold that attacks the fungus and could wipe out the crop in two days. It is time for the smallest ants, the fourth species, to step in and fight the invaders. Under their chin they carry bacteria that produce an antibiotic named Streptomyces, the same microbes that produce Streptomycin for humans. They use this successfully to destroy the enemy mold. These bacteria not only conquer the enemy but also stimulate the growth of the fungus.

Leaf-cutter ants can accomplish two things that human technology cannot. They can grow a single crop year after year without disaster, and they can use an antibiotic so wisely that a harmful bacteria doesn't build up immunity to it. As a result of recent discoveries, researchers are wondering how much remains to be discovered about the world's insects, plants, and animals.[31]

A beetle in the arid Namib Desert of southwest Africa solves the water problem in an unusual way. It stands on its head, causing the moisture of the morning fog it collects on its body to flow down to its mouth.

A rhinoceros beetle is a champion weight lifter. One supported 850 times its own weight on its back. That would be equivalent to our carrying 127,000 pounds.

The white moth feeds on mulberry leaves, which are rich in just the right amount of a milk-like substance and wax. The female lays her eggs on one of these leaves. When the two-inch worm that hatches exudes the milk and wax, it hardens as spun silk when it hits the air. One worm can spin 1,000 feet of silk around its body.

The dragonfly (we used to call it a darning needle) would be an optometrist's delight; it has 30,000 lenses in each eye. As the sun shines on the eye, hitting each lens at a different angle, it enables the fly to remember its directions. It has no difficulty seeing 40 feet away. No wonder.

Butterflies are the most environmentally vulnerable creatures on earth, yet they have survived for millennia to delight admirers. Would you believe there are butterflies

> ...with multifaceted, compound eyes, who see a fourth primary color that is invisible to humans, who eat with their proboscis but taste food with their feet, who use their antennae for feeling, smelling, and hearing? Their senses are said, in many ways, to be superior to humans'.[32]

When a person uses a needle from an AIDS victim, he or she runs the risk of contracting the HIV virus. For this reason, pre-used needles in the drug community have often proved to be a one-way ticket to the mortuary. When a mosquito bites a person with AIDS, then bites someone who is "clean," (that is, free of the virus), there is no danger of transmitting the disease. Think of the worldwide panic that would ensue if mosquitoes could transmit that deadly virus. They can and do transmit malaria, but this disease can usually be treated effectively. With AIDS it's different. There is no known cure. It is a divine mercy and providence that protects people from becoming HIV positive through a mosquito bite.

Protective devices[33]

The old axiom that a good offense is the best defense is certainly true in the case of the skunk. This small black and white mammal mounts a powerful offense with its pungent stench. At close quarters it makes us gag. Other stinkers are the civet cat, the moonrat, the zorilla, the ratel, and the musk turtle. (Most of us will never contact any of these.)

Animals with horns and antlers know how to use them to good advantage in discouraging would-be attackers. Wolves treat a healthy buffalo with healthy respect.

Teddy bears almost always look cute, but the paws and claws of a grizzly bear pack a deadly punch. Its strength is awesome. One dragged a 1,500 pound moose for a mile. Badgers, kangaroos, felines, and ostriches also defend themselves with their claws.

The size of the blue whale, the planet's largest animal, is enough to intimidate smaller sea creatures. The massive hulk of an elephant commands fear. In a zoo it may appear harmless, but some zookeepers have been trampled to death after a powerful switch of its trunk.

Some creatures have teeth as their best weapon. The wolf and tiger lead the pack in this regard. But no one should underestimate the piranha and the shark. Piranhas cause more obituaries than sharks.

Other Miscellaneous Wonders

It's fascinating to study birds, beasts, and fish that are

experts in camouflage. They change color and markings to match their background. Chameleons share their name with people who easily change their principles or opinions according to the prevailing culture. Fawns are hard to discover unless they move. By mimicking a monarch butterfly, the viceroy butterfly looks less appetizing to birds; monarchs are not a blue plate special in a bird's diet. There is a kind of octopus new to science that can mimic more than a dozen other sea creatures. It can resemble the shape of a flounder and move across the sand in an undulating motion. It can float like a jellyfish by looping its arms. It can act like a jawfish by burying itself in the sand with only its eyes showing. It is not clear whether its mimicry is to ward off predators or to deceive potential prey.

God never runs out of good ideas. He creates turtles, armadillos, and shellfish with their own armor. Have you ever tried to pry open a clamshell with your bare hands?

The cheetah's speed is ten miles faster than the antelope's 60 miles per hour. The albatross can gear up to 90 mph.

The electric eel is shocking. With its 200 to 300 volts, it can kill some creatures and stun a human. Catfish and rays have to be satisfied with lower voltage.

When the glass snake is in danger, it jettisons its tail. As the abandoned appendage continues to squirm and wiggle and coil, the predator is so preoccupied and charmed that the snake is able to escape. But what about the tail? Not to worry. The snake soon grows a new one.

The porcupine carries off honors among creatures with quills and spines. Dogs that have had an encounter with one know that the quills enter the nose and mouth more easily than they come out.

God has equipped the rattlesnake with a venomous sting. Some fish and mammals use radar and sonar to locate their enemies. Others are expert in high jumping and gliding. The red fox eludes by running in crazy directions. The opossum just plays dead. There is seemingly endless variety and ingenuity in the provision of protective devices.

But then there are those silly sheep out on the hillsides, some of the most defenseless and clueless of all creatures. Has God forgotten them? No. That's what shepherds are for. And Jesus is our Shepherd. He is our defense. There is none better.

Vegetation

A seed is a remarkable plant in embryo. It contains parts that will develop into root, stem, leaves, and flowers or fruit. All it needs in order to germinate is air, moisture, the right temperature, and suitable illumination. Some seeds have remained dormant for half a century, then when planted, they germinated.

Ten water hyacinths can multiply to more than 600,000 in a single growing season. That is why they have been called "the world's most exotic nuisance."

A giant cactus, known as saguaro, can store enough water to last it for two years of total drought. But it needs a nurse plant to provide shade in summer and warmth in winter during the first 20 or 30 years of its life.

In the Andes a relative of the pineapple lives for 100 years, bursts into bloom, scatters millions of seeds, then dies.

The bristlecone pines of Arizona and Nevada are the oldest known living things on earth. They are gnarled and twisted, but awesome when you stand before them and realize they were growing when Joseph was on earth.

The General Sherman redwood tree has a girth of 79 feet (24 m) and a height of 260 feet (79 m).

The baobab tree of West Africa stores 22,000 gallons

(100,000 liters) of water during the rainy season. During the summer it sheds its leaves to limit evaporation. Then when rain comes, it bursts forth with large white flowers. Its pulp and leaves are good for human consumption, and its bark is used to make rope.

The leaf of a giant water lily in tropical South America is strong enough to bear the weight of a child.

By sending out a particular fragrance at night, the honeysuckle attracts the hawk moth, which is the only insect with a needle snout long enough to go down into its narrow tube. In the process of enjoying the sweet nectar, the moth receives a dusting of pollen, which it then carries to the next honeysuckle it visits.

One species of orchid tricks male bees to visit by imitating the scent of the female bee. It even imitates the shape and color of the female. The male stays long enough for the orchid to deposit two sacs of pollen on its back, which it carries to the next orchid it is duped into visiting.

Every kind of fig is pollinated by its own particular species of wasp. The common fig bears three different types of figs in succession: spring, summer, autumn. Each type is pollinated by three generations of the same wasps. Female wasps lay their eggs inside the fig and then die. The second generation, male and female, mate, and then the males die. The females lay their eggs and thus produce a third generation.

The sausage tree in the south of Africa has something that is used by the people to treat skin cancer. Pharmaceutical companies are taking a lesson from the nationals.

We all know that trees take in carbon dioxide and give out oxygen. If this process were reversed we would all be in deep trouble.

A devotional writer, Aletha Lindstrom, titled her poetry book *Who Tells the Crocuses It's Spring?* It's a good question that could be asked of other "automatic" marvels of creation.

When a tomato plant is attacked by the beet army worm, the injury causes the plant to manufacture several chemicals. Some of them weaken the worm, though not fatally, while others send forth a fragrance. The perfume attracts a particular wasp which needs the worms as food for its larvae. Now the plant is spared to produce tomatoes for our salad.

Bacteria[34]

Bacteria are microscopic organisms that live in soil, water, organic matter, and also in the bodies of people, plants, and animals. Some are beneficial to us, others not so welcome.

We might think that things so tiny would have a simple structure, but it is not so. The more closely they are examined, the more complex they appear. A single bacterial cell can have as much activity as a great metropolis. Thus the God of the telescope is also the God of the microscope.

Bacteriologists are amazed to find that some of these miniscule organisms can survive in the most unlikely environments. They find some in hot water heaters and others in the hot springs of Yellowstone National Park. Others are at home in the acidic springs near volcanoes or in the acid of the human stomach. Amazingly, some live in water that is 23 degrees above the Fahrenheit boiling point. Still others are at home in the Great Salt Lake.

Scientists have found some as deep as 6.8 miles in the ocean. The enormous pressure at that level doesn't crush them. In some places the water is as cold as 39 degrees Fahrenheit. Incredible as it seems, there are bacteria in the frozen waters of the Antarctic.

Some bacteria live best in water that has a low amount of

oxygen. The deeper the water, the less oxygen. The trouble is that gravity won't take bacteria down to their ideal environment, but God has a solution to that problem. They absorb iron particles, arrange them properly, and become living magnets. Their internal compass points them away from the surface and they navigate to lower levels.

Most bacteria can live only in places for which God fitted them. They die quickly if removed from their native habitat.

Many bacteria have a tiny rotor engine with a propeller, which allows them to swim. That incredibly complex motor operates by a flow of acid. It is made of at least 20 different proteins, and 30 more are used in its construction, functioning, and maintenance.

Pardon Our Ignorance

How dare we be proud? *Homo sapiens* prides himself on his marvelous discoveries, his clever inventions, and his record-breaking feats. He has climbed the highest mountain, explored the continents, plumbed the depths of the oceans, and walked on the moon. We have gone from carts to cars to planes and now to space ships. Computers and the Internet are becoming an integral part of modern life.

Man be not proud. It was God who gave us our mind. It is He who puts wisdom in the mind. He times each discovery and each cure for disease. Without Him we could do nothing inventive, certainly not determine the date of the next scientific breakthrough.

It was God who made Michelangelo an artistic genius and Einstein a mental genius. It was the Creator of the atom who determined when human beings would be allowed to split it.

If we are honest we have to admit we have nothing we did not receive (1 Cor. 4:7). We can do nothing unless the ability is given to us from above (Jn. 19:11). These realizations should bring us down to size.

- We know what gravity does; we don't know what it is.
- We don't know what life is, although we experience it day by day.
- Why do the sun and stars burn as slowly as they do?
- Why does the universe expand at the rate it does?
- Why is the universe set up in such a precise, delicate, improbable way?
- Why do atoms hold together as they do, not tighter, nor looser?

Hydrogen is highly inflammable. Oxygen is necessary for combustion. Yet when two parts of hydrogen are combined with one part of oxygen, the result is water—a splendid fire extinguisher. How come?

When it is time for the green turtles of Brazil to mate and lay their eggs, they travel a long distance to Ascension Island in the South Atlantic. We don't know why they go to that particular place or how an inner compass gets them there.

How do some animals know when an earthquake is about to occur? We don't.

If the truth were told, what we know about the natural realm is infinitesimal. Yet how wonderful it is that in the spiritual realm we have in the Bible all we need to know with regard to faith and morals.

Exceptions

Sometimes it seems as if the Lord likes to upset the comfortable theories of men and women by introducing quirky exceptions to the customary order of things. For instance, there's a bird that cannot fly, one that can fly in reverse, and others that can walk under water. Add to that a snake and fish that can fly.

There's an African fish that carries its eggs in its mouth until they're ready to hatch, an extraordinary example of maternal dedication.

School children know that there must be a mommy and daddy if there are going to be little ones, yet virgin birth is found among bees, turkeys, worms, and certain fish, shellfish, and insects. That phenomenon provoked Matt Ridley to write a magazine article titled, "Why Should Males Exist?" Dandelions and other plants are without sex. Some creatures can be bisexual. The Creator does not produce with cookie-cutter sameness.

The duckbilled platypus takes the cake for being an animal oddity. As its name suggests, it has a bill instead of a nose. It has ears curiously located behind the eyes. Unlike other animals in the divine zoo, it lays eggs, has webbed feet, and behind the rear ankles it has poisonous spurs that can be lethal. In some ways this mammal is more like a bird or a reptile.

All metals are solid substances at room temperature. Right? No, wrong. Mercury is a metal and it is liquid at room temperature. We can be thankful for that, because if it were solid, it would not serve in a thermometer or barometer.

Noah had a lot of strange creatures in his ark, and the Lord has amazing variety in His world. The trick for us is to allow for diversity and live in harmony.

CONCLUSION

The wonders of God in creation are inexhaustible. Everything from the starry universe to the living cell is a world of marvels. We see only the fringe of God's work. The Psalmist said that the heavens declare His glory and the firmament shows His handiwork. He could have said this of everything that came from the hand of God.

When we think of the vastness, order, and complexity of creation it is beyond rational belief that it all happened by chance. To claim that man could evolve from primordial slime is absurd.

The theory of evolution is bankrupt. It does not provide a reasonable explanation for the origin of the species. It does not explain the origin of the sexes.

It does not explain the absence of transitional forms, that is, the missing links between species. Although there are changes within a species or "kind," there are no transfers from one species to another. A frog may change its color but it can never become a barracuda. Species always reproduce after their kind.

It overlooks what Einstein called the most validated, immutable, universal law of nature: the law of universal decay and disorder. The Second Law of Thermodynamics, briefly stated, says that things tend to unwind, revert, and deteriorate. There is no advance from one state to another.

The theory of evolution also fails to take into account that in order for a living organism to function, it must be complete. It would not do for vital organs or limbs to be added gradually. An organism requires all its vital parts at one time in order for it to function properly.

The possibility that everything came into being by random chance is so remote statistically that it is unworthy of serious consideration.

The theory of evolution overlooks the fact that intelligent design demands an Intelligent Designer.

The fossil record does not support evolution.

The facts of life do not support the survival of the fittest. We have already mentioned that butterflies, the most environmentally vulnerable of all creatures, have survived for millennia.

Mark Looy of the Institute for Creation Research said it well: "The world around us is so incredibly complex that it cries out for an Intelligent Designer." Looy is a Christian.[35]

Every once in a while we read of a non-believing scientist who acknowledges God. In his book, *The Road Less Traveled and Beyond,* doctor-author M. Scott Peck writes:

> As a scientist, I expect statistical proof whenever possible to convince me of most things. But as I continue to mature, I've become more and more impressed by the frequency of statistically highly improbable events. In their very improbability, I began to see the fingerprint of God.[36]

In recent years a number of distinguished scientists have expressed increasing doubts concerning neo-Darwinian evolution. Michael Denton's book, *Evolution: A Theory in Crisis,* sent shock waves throughout the scientific community. It was a challenge to orthodox Darwinism. He said that evolution "is still, as it was in Darwin's time, a highly speculative hypothesis entirely without direct factual support."[37]

Writing in the *Washington Post*, Eugene F. Mallove said,

> Some scientists are awestruck by the numerous improbable physical coincidences in the universe, without which life could not exist.

Biochemist Michael Behe says that Darwin's theory has "absolutely broken down." In his book, *Darwin's Black Box,* he shows that the human cell is composed of several well-matched, interacting parts, all of which are necessary for the cell to function. This means that the cell could not have developed in evolutionary stages. It had to begin as a functioning cell, and this points to intelligent design. Behe uses a mousetrap to illustrate the point. All five parts must be there to catch a mouse.[38]

Sir Fred Hoyle, renowned astronomer, wrote in *Nature* magazine:

> The chance that higher life forms might have emerged in this way [by evolution] is comparable with the chance that a tornado sweeping through a junk-yard might assemble a Boeing 747 from the material therein.[39]

Atheist Francis Crick, Nobel Prize-winner, once wrote:

> An honest man, armed with all the knowledge available to us now, could only state that in some sense, the origin of life appears at the moment to be almost a miracle, so many are the conditions which would have had to have been satisfied to get it going.[40]

Crick, Carl Sagan, and L. M. Murkhin estimated that the difficulty of evolving a human by chance processes alone is one in $10^{-2,000,000,000}$. According to Borel's law, this is no chance at all.[41]

Even Darwin had grave doubts about his theory. He said that it was "grievously hypothetical." He said, "The eye to this day gives me a cold shudder." To think that it evolved by natural selection was "absurd in the highest possible degree." The likelihood of even a peacock's feather evolving by chance "makes me sick," he said.[42]

It is not surprising that more than a few persons in the scientific community use lavish praise in their observation of nature. In their own words, the wonders there are awesome, incredible, utterly amazing, overwhelming, and staggering to the human mind. One said, "It is surprising that we are not more surprised." Paul Davies said that the impression of design is overwhelming and described the design as "exceedingly ingenious." What we see is "providentially crafted." Use of the term *intelligent design* is not uncommon but use of the capital letters is.

Some of these men come close to acknowledging God as the intelligent designer, but that is where they stop. It is one thing to reject the theory of evolution as a mass of conjecture, and another to let God's foot inside the door. The reason is this. If there is a God, then men and women are responsible to Him, and they don't want this accountability. Even if evolution is discredited, most evolutionists are unwilling to accept the alternative: creation.

The hypothesis of evolution flourished in the days of scientific ignorance, but since the electron microscope came into use and biochemists saw the complexity of the human cell, bacteria, and microbes, evolutionists have scrambled for some explanation that would support their theory and disprove intelligent design. In his book *The Blind Watchmaker,* Richard Dawkins said that "biology is the study of complicated things that give the appearance of being designed for a purpose."[43] Another was so frustrated that he condemned "the boundless stupidity" of nature by making a case for intelligent design.[44]

In *The End of Christendom* Malcolm Muggeridge wrote:

> I myself am convinced that the theory of evolution, especially to the extent to which it has been applied, will be one of the greatest jokes in the history books of the future. Posterity will marvel that so very flimsy and dubious an hypothesis could be accepted with the incredible credulity it has.[45]

PART II

GOD'S WONDERFUL PROVIDENCE

Confide ye aye in Providence,
For Providence is kind:
An' bear ye a' life's changes
Wi' a calm an' tranquil mind.
Tho' pressed and hemmed on every side,
Ha'e faith, an' ye'll win through:
For ilka blade o' grass
Keeps its ain drap o' dew.

JAMES BALLENTINE

GOD'S WONDERFUL PROVIDENCE[1]

Providence is
the almighty and ever present power of God
by which He upholds, as with His hand,
heaven
and earth
and all creatures,
and so rules them that
leaf and blade,
rain and drought,
fruitful and lean years,
food and drink,
health and sickness,
prosperity and poverty—
all things, in fact, come to us
not by chance,
but from His fatherly hand.
—*Heidelberg Catechism*

OLD TESTAMENT EXAMPLES OF GOD'S PROVIDENCE

The Bible is the best book on the providence of God. We see Him working in behalf of His people in breathtaking ways. His timing is perfect. His arranging of circumstances is stellar. He is the divine Chess Player, moving the pieces on the board in the way that is guided by wisdom, power, and love.

In his book *The History of Providence,* Alexander Carson writes:

> Providence is the hand of God ruling the world. God does His will through the voluntary actions of men, and effects His purpose as well by His enemies as by His friends; and through the disobedience and ignorance of His people, as well as through their obedience and knowledge. To account for this is beyond the reach of human intellect. Proud man tries to fathom the abyss, and when he fails, he relieves himself by denying its existence. He will not receive both parts of the truth, but…will modify one of them so as to suit the other, that he may glory that he is able to discover the deep things of the unsearchable God. What he cannot comprehend, with him cannot be true. Will vain man never cease to strive with the Almighty? Will he never learn that the ways of God are inscrutable? *'O the depth of the riches both of the wisdom and knowledge of God! How unsearchable are His judgments and His ways past finding out.'*[2]

Now let us look at a few outstanding examples of His providence in the Old Testament, paying attention to His originality and variety.

Abraham's Offering of Isaac (Gen. 22).

Abraham's willingness to sacrifice Isaac is one of the most heart-wrenching incidents in Bible history. God had asked him to offer his beloved son Isaac as a burnt offering. That meant nothing less than that his unique son would be totally consumed by fire.

Just as that emotion-tossed father was about to plunge a

knife into the heart of the dearest object of his life, a Voice told him to stop. It was the Angel of the Lord, God's own Son in a preincarnate appearance.

Something or Someone caused Abraham to turn around. *Voila!* There was a ram whose horns had trapped him in the bushes. Abraham took the ram and offered it in the place of Isaac.

God had provided! Abraham named the place *The-Lord-Will-Provide.* If this had happened today He might call it *Mount Providence.*

Isaac and Rebekah (Gen. 24).

Abraham's servant went to Mesopotamia to find a wife for Isaac. One evening as he sat by a well outside the city of Nahor, he asked the Lord to reveal the right woman in a specific way: If she not only gave him a drink of water but also offered to draw water for the camels, she would be the right wife for Isaac. Many women came to the well but only Rebekah met the requirements. The Lord had led the servant as to how to pray for guidance, then He led him to meet Rebekah and ask for a drink, and finally he led Rebekah as to what to say and do. Thus God provided a wife for Isaac and wrote another chapter in the bloodline of the Messiah.

Joseph (Gen. 37-50).

The Lord had told Abraham that his descendants would be displaced from Canaan and would be slaves in a foreign land for 400 years. Finally they would exit that land with great possessions (Gen. 15:13-14). Then He brought that promise to pass in an ingenious way through a young fellow named Joseph. This lad's jealous brothers plotted to kill him, but finally relented and sold him to a caravan of traders. This is how Joseph got a free trip to Egypt. There an officer of Pharaoh bought him and for a while he prospered in his new environment, but then his master's wife falsely accused him of attempted rape, and he landed in prison. Had God's program failed?

No, while in prison Joseph demonstrated that he could interpret dreams. So when Pharaoh had a dream that his astrologers could not explain, word reached him that a prisoner named Joseph could help.

Released from prison, Joseph revealed that a worldwide famine was coming and suggested a masterful plan for dealing with it. His administrative skill advanced him to second place in the kingdom.

When the famine reached Canaan, Joseph's brothers had to make three trips to Egypt for food. Their father Jacob and all the family were in the last entourage. Joseph settled them in the rich pastureland of Goshen, the garden spot of Egypt.

After Joseph died, a new Pharaoh made slaves of the Israelites and refused to release them, but his will was broken in the night of the Passover. Israel escaped, taking great possessions with them, as God had predicted to Abraham.

Moses (Ex. 2)

Often when God is going to do something important, a baby is born. In this instance the baby's name was Moses. To escape the murderous edict of the Pharaoh, his mother set him adrift in a basket. Was it a coincidence that the ruler's daughter came down to the river to bathe at just that time? Perhaps it was a baby's cry that directed her attention to a basket in the bulrushes. Her compassion surfaced. But instead of taking the baby back to the palace, she promised to pay a local woman to care for him. As it turned out, the local woman was Moses' mother.

Big doors swing on little hinges.

Ruth (Ruth 1–4)

Meet a Jewish couple, Elimelech and Naomi, and their two sons, Mahlon and Chilion. Famine caused them to move from Bethlehem in Canaan to Gentile Moab, a questionable move. The sons married Gentile brides, Ruth and Orpah, and then the father and the two young husbands died.

When Naomi determined to return home, Ruth vowed to go with her. It was the beginning of the barley harvest when they reached Bethlehem.

When an Israelite died, it was important that the land remain in the family and that there be posterity to carry on the family name. A near relative was supposed to marry the widow.

Never one to be idle, Ruth went to glean in a field of barley. It so happened that the field belonged to a man named Boaz, and it so happened that Boaz was a relative of Naomi's late husband.

Boaz was willing to be Ruth's kinsman-redeemer but there was a legal complication; a closer relative had a prior claim on her. When the closer relative chose not to redeem Ruth, Boaz did. Through this union Ruth became the grandmother of David and thus an ancestress of the Lord Jesus.

Esther (Esther 1–10)

In the story of Esther we find what J. G. Bellett called

> …the wonderful interweaving of circumstances. There is plot and counterplot, wheels within wheels, circumstances hanging upon circumstances, all formed together to work out the wonderful plans of God.

Those were designed coincidences. Not one happened by chance.

A captive Jewish maiden won a royal beauty contest and married a Gentile king, a highly irregular circumstance. Her cousin Mordecai heard of a plot against the king, notified Esther, and the king's life was spared. There was not a word of thanks. There was no reward.

A scoundrel named Haman talked the king into signing an unalterable decree to exterminate the Jews. Lots were cast to determine the execution date. It was a year away (God controlled the lot).

It was clear that Esther must appear before the king to intercede for her people and for herself, but there was a complication. If she entered the king's presence and he did not hold out his scepter to her, she was doomed to die. It is not sure that he would hold out the scepter, because he and the queen had not been together for 30 days.

Esther bit the bullet and stood before the king. He did hold out his scepter and asked what she wanted. Her request seemed rather lame, unrelated to the crisis at hand. All she wanted was to invite the king and Haman to a banquet. Why didn't she come to the point?

At the banquet she seemed to diddle still further. She asked the king and Haman to come to a second banquet. Haman was overjoyed. But on the way home he became furious because Mordecai wouldn't bow to him, so he ordered a gallows to be built for the obstinate Jew.

In between the two banquets, the monarch had a king-sized case of insomnia. He ordered the history of his reign to be brought. Of all the books in the library, they happened to bring the one that recorded the story of how Mordecai had revealed a plot against the ruler. That was the right time for Esther's cousin to be honored, much to Haman's chagrin.

At the dinner, Esther exposed Haman as the enemy of her people, and the king responded by ordering his death.

Someone suggested that there was a gallows nearby, the one that Haman had built for Mordecai. Haman was speedily dispatched.

But the unchangeable decree for the extermination of the Jews still stood. True, it could not be changed, but a new decree could be passed, permitting the Jews to defend themselves. Now they had had a year in which to arm themselves (Esther 3:7; 9:1). The Lord had wonderfully provided for their deliverance. They defended themselves with great aplomb, and ever since their victory has been celebrated with the Feast of Purim.

Daniel and His Friends (Dan. 1-6)

Daniel and his three friends put their careers in the Babylonian kingdom on the line by refusing to eat non-kosher food from the royal kitchen. By this refusal to compromise they excelled in appearance, wisdom, and knowledge, and won promotion at the court.

When none of his astrologers could interpret the king's dream, Daniel stepped forward and explained it in detail. This brought him even greater promotion.

Later, when the king demanded that everyone should bow to his golden image, Shadrach, Meshach, and Abednego drew a line in the sand, and for their disobedience, they spent a night in a furnace of fire. But the Lord was with them in the furnace, and they emerged unharmed. Not even the smell of smoke was on them. Only the ropes that bound them were consumed.

The only way Daniel's jealous enemies could find guilt in him was by passing a law forbidding prayer to anyone but the king. Daniel preferred to be in a den of lions rather than to stop praying to God. His situation seemed hopeless but God clamped the jaws of the lions, and they were harmless as kittens.

Jonah

When the disobedient prophet Jonah wanted to flee from the presence of the Lord, a ship was waiting at the pier to take him to Tarshish. Very convenient. When everything seemed to be going his way, a storm descended on the ship, causing terror and despair. Not so convenient. When the crew sought a reason for the storm, the lot fell on Jonah. God was speaking. Even when Jonah was thrown into the sea, a great fish was waiting to swallow him. God's voice was getting louder. Later when the prophet pouted over God's mercy to Nineveh, the Lord prepared a plant with huge leaves to protect him from the sun. The Lord is gracious.

All history is the record of the providence of God, whether we see it or not. Sometimes it is more obvious than at other times, but He is always there, keeping watch over His own. Now let us turn to see how He has shown Himself strong on behalf of believers in more recent times.

HE LED THEM SAFELY[3]

Robert and Ellen Stephen sensed that the Lord was guiding them to leave Scotland and serve Him in China—in Shantung, to be specific. Both came from strong Bible backgrounds; they had read and studied the Bible, and had memorized great portions of it. That fact is an important part of the story.

At times Ellen was seized with fear concerning their step of faith. After all, her husband was only 23 years old. The future was filled with unknowns. So one night Ellen asked the Lord for some word of assurance, some promise that would set her spirit at rest. Almost immediately she was impressed with Psalm 78:53. She couldn't get it out of her mind: *"And He led them on safely so that they did not fear."*

They left Peterhead and stopped off in Glasgow on the first lap of their journey. At a meeting there, they met the saintly Andrew Bonar, who gave them the priestly blessing of Aaron (Num. 6:24-26). Then kindly laying his hand on Ellen's shoulder, he said, "When your husband is itinerating, you may often be left alone, but remember, *'He led them on safely so that they feared not.'"*

While in Glasgow they stayed with Mr. and Mrs. Robert Barnett, then moved on to Bath, England, where they stayed with Dr. and Mrs. Maclean. Framed over the mantelpiece was Ellen's verse (Ps. 78:53).

The next stop was a city named Leominster where Mrs. Yapp was their hostess. On the last day, she happened to ask Mrs. Stephen whether her mother was still living. Ellen explained that she had died three months earlier. Taking the outgoing missionary into her arms, Mrs. Yapp said, "The Lord was gracious to your mother, but don't grieve, dear. *'He led them on safely so that they feared not.'"*

Then on to London and Tilbury where they would embark for China. Quite a few Christians had come to see them off. One lady whose name Ellen never knew handed her a slip of paper with Psalm 78:53 scribbled on it.

As the ship slowly moved away from the dock, a man made a megaphone with his hands and called, *"He led them on safely so that they feared not."*

The ocean voyage was uneventful until they reached Hong Kong, but then a typhoon buffeted them for three days—and a baby boy was born to Robert and Ellen.

At Shanghai, Mr. Stephen asked the captain if he could leave his wife and his baby on board while he went ashore to locate a hospital. The captain had a better idea.

"I'll send you all ashore in the Customs launch."

Then noticing another launch approaching, he corrected,

"No, I'll send you on that one; they are your kind of people."

The gangplank was lowered and a man came aboard. After greeting the captain, he faced Robert and said, "Is your name by any chance Stephen?"

"It is, but who are you, if I might ask?"

"My name is Tom. You and your wife stayed with my brother-in-law in Glasgow. Go and get your wife and I'll take you ashore."

Robert explained that their family was now three and he would be grateful if Tom could direct them to a hospital.

"Hospital? Hospital? You don't want a hospital. I've got a wife and a home; go and tell your wife she has nothing to fear. Get her ready and I'll go ashore and get an ambulance."

Soon the Stephen family was comfortably settled in the home of Tom and his wife. When Ellen went to bed that night, she saw a familiar verse of Scripture on the wall. Yes, it was Psalm 78:53: *"He led them on safely so that they feared not."*

Many years later, after Ellen had gone home to be with the Lord, her daughter Lois wrote:

My mother wanted that verse to be the Lord's own message to her. She told no one of the apparent coincidences. But through riots, the Boxer rising, much serious illness on my father's part, and through a mutiny and civil war, nothing moved my mother's faith, and she was a *'strong tower'* to us all. Failing health did not shake her, and it was when she knew she was going to leave that she told me the whole story. What it has meant to me, you can imagine!

TALK ABOUT CAR TROUBLE!

In assembling stories of the wonderful way in which the

Lord provides for His people under the most unlikely circumstances, I was struck by the number of stories that featured auto crises. Here is one that leaves us emotionally exhausted when we think of the roadblocks that arose and the ingenuity of the Lord in removing them.

David and Eleanor Long were missionaries in one of the most primitive and isolated spots in Angola. Eleanor was an expectant mother and it was necessary for them to travel to Boma for medical attention.

The child wasn't expected until February, but December and January were rainy months when the roads were a sea of mud, the rivers were swollen, and the makeshift bridges often floated away. Their pick-up vehicle was seven years old and the trip would be between 540 and 650 miles, depending on which dirt track they took.

About six weeks before their planned departure, David had to drive to Malange for much needed supplies. On the way back, the overloaded truck began misfiring, overheating, and losing power.

David let it cool down for a while, restarted it, and drove the last few miles home with the car stuttering and jerking. Not knowing the real problem, David stripped down the whole unit. So far, so good. But when he reassembled the parts, he didn't reseat the oil pump properly. He confidently installed a new cylinder head gasket and started the engine, but when he did, the pump fell out of place and the crankshaft drove it out through the side of the engine block, leaving a gaping hole.

Now what to do? There were no auto parts stores, no repair service garages, no cars like this one anywhere in the district. The possibility of finding a compatible engine block was practically nil. And even if he could find another engine, he had no money to buy it and no mechanic to install it. The outlook was grim. It was the worst predicament in their five years of African frustrations. The dreaded solution would be for Eleanor to be carried in a hammock to Boma—14 uncomfortable days through flooded plains, swollen rivers, and sleeping in a tent each night.

David and Eleanor sent up desperate distress calls to the Lord. It would be interesting to see how He would solve this dilemma.

The chariot wheels of God began to turn. The Government Administrative Officer at the Post summoned two mechanics from Bie to overhaul the engine of his own car and also to see what could be done for the Longs. When the men saw the gaping hole in the engine, they threw up their hands, ruefully announced that only a new engine block would do, and departed.

Then the Lord jiggled the memory of one of the mechanics. At Bie they had once recovered the remains of a Ford that had had an encounter with a train. The chassis was totaled, but the engine was intact. He had towed it away, thinking that some parts might be recovered and sold. Mr. Long could have the engine block for $100.

Now there were two more problems. How could David get it from Bie, and how could he pay for it? He didn't have the money. The Post officer said that he would send a roadwork gang to Bie and that they could carry it back, lashed to poles. It would take a week for them to get to Bie, and two weeks for them to pack and return. It was one of the most painful moments in David's life when he had to admit that he did not have the money to pay for it. He and Eleanor had come to the mission field living by faith, having no visible means of support, and looking to the Lord alone for the supply of their needs. Yet here was an engine that he needed so desperately, probably the only engine of that kind in all Angola.

Again the official sought to help. He offered to lend the

money, payable whenever it was convenient. But this would be against the Longs' faith principles. David explained: "We do not receive a regular salary but are supported by Christians and living by faith in God, and we have no idea if and when such a sum might come."

Both David and the officer knew that mail came at best every two weeks, and frequently with gaps of two months. "After some coaxing that we should accept and let him send the men immediately, I had to let them go back to the Post while Eleanor and I sat down and wept."

Two days later the Officer came excitedly to the Longs and announced that a runner had come with official papers from his superior. Among the papers was an overseas letter for the Longs. It was a mystery how the letter had gotten mixed up with the official papers.

The officer urged them to open the letter without delay. He was positive that it contained money. David was numb with fear and embarrassment. Suppose there was no money in it. What a loss of face.

In the letter was a check for $120, one of the largest gifts the missionaries had received during their time in Africa. The officer felt vindicated. He offered to change the money into Escudos, giving the Longs a better rate of exchange than they could get elsewhere. And he immediately made plans to bring the engine from Bie.

The engine was then wrapped in tarpaulin, slung onto a pole with three cross bars carried by six men. Six other men went ahead with axes to cut out shrubs and trees and thus widen the path, and six walked along until it was their turn to carry the load.

Before the engine's arrival, some men pushed the Longs' pick-up for five miles, mostly uphill, from their house to the Post. There the mechanics took out the old engine and stripped all the parts off the block so that when the "new" engine arrived, they could assembly everything quickly.

Three weeks later the exhausted men arrived with the engine block. The mechanics swung into action, working day and night to put it all together. When they had tested it, they turned it over to the Longs.

Without delay the missionaries packed their things and left for Boma. The mud was so deep that after four days they had to stop at Bie. They left the pick-up there, took the train to Luso where Dr. Bier, a fellow missionary, met them and drove them to Boma.

Their calculations as to the timing of the baby's arrival were wrong. As David said later: "We had to wait a week or two while the good doctor drove Eleanor over every bumpy road and rickety bridge with extra doses of quinine to try to speed things up a bit."

Finally on the last day of February the baby arrived. David commented: "I have wondered if my son realizes what he put us through."

THE GUMMED-UP CARBURETOR

Some car troubles require a whole lot of prayer and a little dose of ingenuity. Dena Speering found this out. She needed both.

One day she left Itendey for Mongbwalu to teach a ladies' Bible Class. As is common on the mission field, when you travel, there is always someone who wants to go with you. This day was no exception. A young national fellow rode with her to the class and then back in the afternoon.

On the homeward trip they had gone about 10 miles when the engine died. Dena didn't know much about auto mechanics but she looked under the hood, having no idea what to look for, or where to find the trouble. But she had watched others take the cap off a gadget, which she later learned was the distributor. Inside she saw a part that had broken in pieces (a rotor). She removed the parts and wrapped them in a Kleenex. This would be diagnostic evidence if anyone came to give her roadside assistance.

By this time the young man was walking the 15 miles to Itendey to get help.

Dena decided to get into the back seat and redeem the time by studying for next week's Bible class. She had barely started when she remembered she had not prayed about this predicament. So she went to the Lord and poured out her heart to him. As soon as she said *Amen*, she felt pangs of hunger, but there was no food. All she had was some gum. So she started chewing some, which gave the illusion of eating something nutritional.

Another brainstorm. Why not look for some glue? It was common to carry glue in a tire repair kit on trips like this. There was no glue, however, so she continued studying.

Then it struck her as an obvious solution. Why not stick the parts of the rotor together with gum? She took all the pieces and carefully pressed them together with the gum. But when she tried to put the repaired rotor back into the distributor, it fell apart.

If at first you don't succeed...she tried again. With great care she stuck the parts together and with even greater care she placed the assembled rotor in the distributor. This time the gummed parts hung together.

Fearing the worst, Dena got in the car and started it. Amazingly it purred like a kitten. She rode the 15 miles back home, picking up would-be riders along the way. The car performed admirably right to her front door.

Later, when they looked into the distributor, the rotor had fallen apart. Not to worry. They were now in a position to order a new one.

Every Need Supplied

The doctors had told Ben Iler that if he didn't get out of Zambia, he would die. Anti-malaria medicines were destroying his liver, so he and his wife Frances decided they must move to South Africa. Everything they owned had to be packed into their pick-up truck. Then they were ready to leave Zambia, travel through Botswana, and get settled in their new home.

On the way, terrorist trucks would roar past them, churn up a cloud of dust, and slow down in front of them. The canopy at the back of the truck would be unzipped and an AK47 would appear, aimed at them. Ben would wave and give them a thumbs up. As soon as the terrorists realized that Ben and Frances were "good guys," they would zipper up the canopy and speed off.

When the Ilers reached Livingstone, they were hungry so they went into a store to get a loaf of bread. The only food on the shelves was Vim, which Ben described as tasting like scouring powder, used for scrubbing pans. They weren't *that* hungry so they drove 25 or 30 more miles to Kazangulu, at the border of Zambia and Botswana.

The border officials were all fairly drunk at that time, but after several tries, they were able to stamp the passports. Ben and Frances proceeded to a pontoon barge that would ferry them and the pick-up across the river to the Botswana immigration and customs area.

There the officials asked for their triptych, a sort of transit visa that indicated that they would only be passing through the country and would not sell anything en route.

The official thundered that the triptych was not valid because it had a wrong engine number, a 7 instead of a 1.

"What do we do now?" Ben asked.

"You'll have to pay customs duty on the vehicle and

everything in it."

"How much would that be?"

After a careful inspection, the man said that it would be 800 Rands (a Rand at that time was a little over $2.00). The Ilers had less than 100 Rands on hand, just enough to buy fuel for the rest of the trip to South Africa.

"What happens if we can't pay this?"

"You can turn around and go back to Zambia right now. Otherwise we will confiscate the truck and its contents tomorrow."

That was a problem. Shortly after the Ilers had used the pontoon barge, the Rhodesians had bombed it out of the water, killing five or six men. There was no way of returning to Zambia.

The customs official gave Ben a 24-hour Temporary Permit, enabling them to find accommodations for the night. On the outskirts of Kasani, they pulled in at a place called Hunter's Lodge, and were given one of the huts. Heather, the owner's wife, was a true believer, and with Christian courtesy she invited the Ilers to supper at seven P.M. It was a meal fit for a king, wild game with all the fixings. They admitted that they stuffed themselves.

While they were sitting in the lounge afterwards, a hunting party came in for a late supper. One of the men came to Ben and said:

"You look like an American."

"Yes, it's hard to hide, isn't it."

"Would you have any American dollars that you would like to sell?"

"Afraid not. We have been in the bush for some time. But I do have a checking account with Chase Manhattan in New York."

"Perfect," the stranger said. "Could you spare me 500 Rands worth of dollars? I'm on my way to New York on three months' vacation. They will allow me only 500 Rands worth of dollars at customs and I would like to double that."

Ben looked at his check book stub and figured that by the time this man reached New York, there would be enough in the account to cover the check, so he wrote out a check. The man gratefully gave 500 Rands to Ben, a total stranger. It was a real act of faith.

That night in their little hut, Ben and Frances fell on their knees and thanked the Lord for the 500 Rands. But they reminded the Lord that it was 800, not 500 that they needed. Then they slept soundly, a miracle in itself.

In the morning they had a sumptuous breakfast. When Ben tried to pay Heather for all her kindness, she said, "Not a penny. We're happy to have missionaries here. Any time you come through, please come and stay with us."

Later that morning, as the Ilers were driving through the gate of the Hunter's Lodge, Ben happened to look in the rear view mirror and saw Heather running after them, waving an envelope. Ben braked and backed up.

She said breathlessly, "You're going to South Africa, aren't you?"

"Well, we're going to try," meaning "if the Lord provides 300 more Rands."

"My three kids are with my mother in Johannesburg, and their tuition and clothing allotment are due. This letter has 300 Rands cash in it. If I mail it from here in Botswana, it will never reach South Africa. Would you mind mailing this when you get to Pretoria?"

"Why certainly, but on one condition. If you let me use those 300 Rands cash, I will see that your mother gets a check as soon as we get to Pretoria. I have a daughter living there."

"Oh," she said, "that's an answer to prayer." Little did she know that it was an answer to the Ilers' prayer also.

Ben now had 800 Rands. He drove straight to the customs office and counted out the money. The officer was amazed—and perhaps disappointed. He and the others had probably already decided how to divide the loot.

The officer blurted out, "How did you ever get that money?"

"The Lord knew our needs before we even got here to Kasani."

The man hung his head and was strangely quiet. Then he put his hand over the counter and said, "Shake hands, brother. I too am a believer."

"Really? When did you receive Christ as your Savior?"

"Many years ago some missionaries came to Bechuana land. I heard the gospel as a little boy and trusted Christ. But I haven't lived for Him."

Ben and Frances had a good talk with him, then left with his blessing. They thought, "Now we are across the Red Sea. Pharaoh and his army are defeated and it will be a smooth trip from now on." Little did they know.

They drove all day to Francistown where they were booked to stay at the Grand Hotel. Ben felt that "Grand" was a misnomer. The little rondovles (cabins) were infested. There wasn't a *single* cockroach; every one of them was married and had a large family.

Maybe they should move on. The gas stations in South Africa closed at noon on Saturday and this was Friday night. So after praying about it, they decided to buy some bread and cheese and drive all night.

The cows in Botswana think that the roads are for them, so they sleep on them, quite oblivious to auto horns. Ben had to dodge them often or get out and plead with them to move.

Just before they got to the border with South Africa, they

pulled off the road and slept, Frances on the front seat and Ben on top of the load.

While he was getting breakfast, Ben turned on the radio. News flash! That very night the Rhodesians had raided the Grand Hotel, had taken three carloads of terrorists, and shot up the place.

Ben asked, "Did the Lord want us to get to South Africa? I have an idea He did. He provided. He knew what was going to happen and saw to it that our lives were preserved."

THE ASIAN WHO DISAPPEARED[4]

In her book *First We Have Coffee,* Margaret Jensen paints a winsome, homespun picture of life in a Norwegian immigrant family. Papa Tweten was engrossed in the Word of God and in preaching it wherever he was led. The mundane things of life meant little to him. Mama Tweten was remarkable for her unspoiled faith, which never became complicated. If God said something, that was enough for her. He cannot lie. He can do anything. He answers prayer. He never fails. It was all so simple.

After they had lived in Winnipeg for some time, Papa was called to serve as a missionary to Scandinavian immigrants throughout the Province of Saskatchewan. So they uprooted and moved in their antiquated car. It was a long journey and although Mama had packed bread and sugared waffles to sustain them, they ran out of food and drink. Mama mentioned how much she would like a cup of coffee and a bowl of soup, so when Papa saw a white cottage in an open field on the outskirts of a town, he stopped and went to the door.

When an Asian man came to the door, Papa explained that they would like to buy a cup of coffee (he didn't mention soup because they didn't have enough money for that). With oriental courtesy and hospitality, the man summoned them to come into a restaurant that adjoined the house. They would have more than a cup of coffee; they would have a complete meal.

He seated them at a table with a white linen cloth. The four children had never been in a restaurant before. There were no other guests in the room. They bowed their heads and gave thanks with a Norwegian blessing. How they enjoyed that meal!

Upon leaving, each one of the Tweten family thanked the gracious host. Papa said, "Some day I will return to repay you for your kindness. May God's richest blessing be upon you."

After they reached Saskatoon and got settled in their new home, Papa took to the road in the service of the King. His missionary journeys covered many miles in all kinds of Canadian weather. He and his family lived off freewill offerings that his "parishioners" gave him. But he had an unsettling way of giving some of the money to needy people he met. God would take care of his family.

There was a long period during which the family didn't hear from him—and Christmas was approaching. Food was scarce. The meal on Christmas Eve was soup and bread. But in the midst of their festivity, a crowd came from their church with boxes of food and gifts. Mama was right; God takes care of His children.

After the church people had left, the family heard boots stomping on the porch. The door opened, and it was Papa. He explained that he had been in a terrible snowstorm and had become disoriented. He prayed and the Lord led him to the light of a prairie cabin where he was cared for until the storm subsided. Christmas day was glorious, with Papa telling of his exploits in the gospel.

Many years later Papa told his daughter Margaret that he had returned to repay the Asian man for his kindness. He knew the location but when he got to it, there was no house, no restaurant. Just an open field. He asked people in the community where he could locate the Asian who ran the restaurant. They all said the same thing. No Asian had ever lived there. There never was a house there in the field, and certainly no restaurant.

Papa said to Margaret, "To Mama and me it was such an awesome thing. We were too full of wonder to speak of it. As the years passed, we became convinced that our host was an angel."

Why should anyone doubt?

QUICK CURE[5]

Answers to prayer were not unusual in the Tweten household. Mama expected them; in fact, she depended on them. Take, for instance, the time that little Gordon was having trouble breathing. Another symptom was that there was a foul odor from his nose. The doctor scheduled nasal surgery in the hospital for the following week.

Back home again, the family gathered for prayer. Mama reminded them of the Savior's promise to answer prayer when it was offered in His name. She said to the Lord, "We ask that the source of this problem be removed, and bless the doctor and the nurses."

God didn't take long in acting. First he moved Gordon to start playing with a can of black pepper. As the little fellow finally succeeded in opening the can, he inhaled a big whiff of it. This brought on an explosive sneeze, resulting in a button being shot from Gordon's nose across the room.

Mama immediately verbalized the lesson of the day: "My God shall supply all your need. Today, children, God supplied surgery through a pepper can. With God all things are possible."

Yes, God certainly has a sense of humor.

ANGELS UNAWARES[6]

We can't put God in a box. If we try, He will outsmart us every time.

From time to time governments have decided to prohibit the entrance of Bibles into their lands. Soon an underground river of Bibles starts to flow, thanks to the work of dedicated smugglers who believe they ought to obey God rather than man.

The files of *Open Doors,* an organization of courageous Bible distributors, contain many stories of how the Lord outfoxed the wrath of man and made it praise Him. Here is one such account.

Two couriers—one Canadian, one Scot—arrived in China on an international flight, each carrying bags heavily loaded with Bibles. Their plan was to change to a domestic flight upon arrival in order to travel deeper into China to their destination city. Because of flight delays, however, once they had successfully cleared the passport and customs posts, the two men found they had only three minutes to make their way to the domestic departure terminal.

They also discovered that the distance between the two buildings would have to be covered by foot.

With darkness fast approaching and rain now pelting down, the two men began to despair. If they missed their connecting flight, they would also miss meeting their contact. Had they come so far only to be left in the dark and rain with their Bibles? The couriers quickly realized they had little alternative but to pray.

After a short prayer, they had barely opened their eyes when a policeman came cycling toward them. With their hands waving, the men indicated to the Chinese official their need to get to the domestic departure terminal as quickly as possible.

The policeman took pity on the wet foreigners, and within a few seconds the Canadian found himself seated squarely behind the official, together with his three bags, heading off toward his flight.

Just as the Scot began wondering if the policeman would arrive back in time to pick him up, another official on a cycle approached. This time it was a customs officer from the international terminal. With the same waving of hands, the visitor quickly found himself and his load of Bibles on the bicycle behind the officer.

The two couriers arrived at the terminal just in time to make their connecting flight. After unloading their bags and gathering their thoughts, they turned around to thank the benevolent Chinese officials.

To their surprise, neither officer was to be seen. Were they angels in disguise? Regardless of who they were and why they had picked them up, the two couriers later laughed over God's sense of humor—and provision.

Once again we are reminded that there is a very thin veil between the visible, physical world and the invisible, spiritual one. God is not limited to flesh and blood.

WARNED TO WITHDRAW

On May 28 the networks blared out the news of another in a series of school shootings. This one was at Thurston High School in Springfield, Oregon. A 15-year-old student entered the school cafeteria with a semiautomatic rifle and two pistols and discharged 51 rounds of ammunition. He fatally injured two students and wounded 18 others. After the police took him into custody, they found he had shot his parents to death before going to the school.

One interesting story of God's providence didn't get into the news broadcasts. Several months before the shooting, a Christian mother, Lois Reichle, felt a strong burden to take her two older children out of the school and teach them at home. Scott was a senior and Kristina a junior. It was not that there was anything especially threatening about the school. Actually it had a very good academic standing. It was a plus for students desiring to go on to college to have "Thurston High School" on their diploma. Sure, there had been some fights on campus, but nothing serious.

There were many reasons why it didn't make sense to take two of her children out of high school a few months before the end of the school year. Scott's diploma would read "Home School" instead of "Thurston." Both he and Kristina would be taken away from their friends. All the relatives raised their eyebrows at what she was doing, and even she herself panicked at the thought of teaching them at home.

But she didn't have peace about leaving her children there. The voice of the Lord was increasingly urgent to both her and her husband. As they weighed their biblical responsibility, Lois finally began to consider God's will rather than her own convenience and comfort zone. As soon as she submitted to the Lord, her fear of home schooling vanished. Both parents decided she would begin in January 1998. The son accepted the decision quite well; the daughter was understandably unhappy. She said, "I'll do it, but I won't like it."

On May 28, they would have been in the cafeteria when the shooting occurred. Now they know that their Mom was right. Her decision saved them from being present when the bullets flew.

How remarkable that God can influence the intellect and will of two of His people to take action that is contrary to conventional wisdom in order to further His purposes.

It does not always work this way, of course. In a later school shooting, it was not God's will to remove a girl from her school. Instead Cassie Bernall was martyred for her fearless confession of the Lord. It is a replay of Acts 12 where James was martyred and Peter was spared.

GOD AT THE HELM[7]

It would be a routine trip from Puerto Maldonado to Jayave. At least that's what missionary Brad Hallock thought as he and two national believers, Luis and Casiano, set out one Wednesday morning in a 30-foot dugout boat with a 25-horsepower motor. First they had to go down the Tambopata River, then join the Madre de Dios, and finally merge into Rio Inambari. It should be a 12-hour trip to carry the Good News to the people at Jayave.

Before they had gone far in the Tambopata, they found that instead of riding with the current, they were battling it. The Madre de Dios was a mighty torrent; it was at flood tide and was backing up into the Tambopata. Logs and trees posed a hazard to navigation.

By nightfall the three men were only a quarter of the way to their destination. They pulled over to the shore, asked permission to camp, set up their tent, and stayed overnight. The next morning they were on their way by six A.M. By lunchtime they reached Laberinto on the Inambari, where they should have been for lunch the previous day.

Three hours upriver they met still more problems. The flood made a particularly treacherous section worse. Waves 2-3 feet high threatened to swamp the boat. Water splashed into the dugout, soaking both passengers and cargo.

Across the river the men spotted a shallow inlet where they could camp, if they could get to it. Brad eased the boat into the current. At full throttle it could barely hold its own against the waves. Sometimes it would slip downstream, then struggle back again. Brad ordered Luis and Casiano to put on their life jackets. When they finally crossed and reached the side channel, the engine coughed and died. What if that had happened in the middle of the river?

Their efforts to start the motor again were futile. The sun was setting and they were tired. Then Brad spotted a trail leading to a gold miner's camp, so they started out to ask permission to camp on his premises. Miners aren't always pleased to see strangers on their property. If this one said no, Brad and his friends might have to paddle upstream for an hour in the dark before reaching another cove.

But this time was different. A man came running down to the trail to meet them. He said excitedly, "You stopped. You finally stopped. I've been waving at you for two years to stop here because my wife and I want to know more about God." What he said about their failure to stop was true. Ordinarily Brad passed by on the other side of the river, hesitant to fight the life-threatening current to see what people wanted.

Quickly the three sailors set up camp, ate a hurried meal, and went to visit with Pascual Tunci and his family. The Tuncis were waiting in the kitchen, warmed by a friendly fire. Brad opened his Bible and told them God's great plan of salvation. Before the evening was over, Pascual, his wife, and a worker made professions of faith in Christ. Brad didn't leave until he had taught them some of the basics of the Christian life.

In the morning, the missionary gave them a Bible and some Christian books, and extracted a few badly decayed teeth. Then it was time to think about the motor. Pascual diagnosed the problem as a bad coil. But not to worry; he had an extra one they could use until they could get a new one. This saved them from floating back to the town of Laberinto, not a pleasure trip in a raging flood.

They set out joyfully and arrived in Jayave at noon on Friday.

It was another great opportunity to share the Word of God with hungry hearts.

As he mused on the trip, Brad commented,

This was certainly different from what I had planned. *"The mind of man plans his ways, but the Lord directs his steps."* I wouldn't have had it any other way. What a joy to be placed by the Lord through circumstances at a place where thirsty hearts are just waiting for someone to bring the news of Living Water.

CAN GOD?[8]

As the Flying Fortress hurtled toward the waters of the Pacific, the navigator suggested that the crew pray. For some this was not a time for prayer; it was a time for quick thinking and speedy action.

On board the B-17 was a crew of five, and three passengers. Bill Cherry was the pilot, Jim Whittaker the copilot, Johnny DeAngelis the navigator, Johnny Bartek the engineer' and Jimmy Reynolds the radioman. The three passengers were Eddie Rickenbacker, Col. Hans Adamson, and Sgt. Alex Kaczmarczyk. The first two were en route to inspect American airfields in the South Pacific. The sergeant was returning to active duty after a bout with hepatitis. It was about 4:30 P.M. on October 21, 1942, when the huge plane smashed into the waves.

After quickly recovering from the jolt, the men inflated three yellow life rafts and abandoned the plane. They had four oranges, some knives, and some fishhooks and line.

On the first night adrift, they saw sharks ominously circling the rafts. By nightfall of the second day, their thirst was intense. The third day out, their craving for water was almost unbearable. Whittaker, the copilot noticed Johnny Bartek reading the New Testament he had carried in his pocket.

By the fourth day, only one orange was left, to be divided among eight men. But then the miracle occurred. A sea swallow landed on Eddie Rickenbacker's head and stayed long enough for the men to capture it. They divided the meat among themselves, and used the innards as bait. The few fish they caught allayed their hunger a little, but their saltiness intensified their thirst.

When Johnny Bartek suggested they have a prayer meeting, Whittaker poured cold water on the idea but Rickenbacker overruled him. So the senior man, Col. Adamson, first read Matthew 6:31-34 from the New Testament:

Therefore do not worry, saying, "What shall we eat?" or "What shall we drink?" or "What shall we wear?" For after all these things the Gentiles seek. For your heaven-

ly Father knows that you need all these things. But seek first the kingdom of God and His righteousness, and all these things shall be added to you. Therefore do not worry about tomorrow, for tomorrow will worry about its own things. Sufficient for the day is its own trouble.

Whittaker cynically suggested that these past few days had had enough in the way of trouble. All he wanted was some food and drink. But the men prayed anyway.

The sixth day began and ended with Bible reading and prayer. Pilot Cherry prayed:

O Master, we know that there isn't a guarantee that we'll eat in the morning. But we're in an awful fix. We sure are counting on a little something by the day after tomorrow, at least. See what You can do, O Master.

The answer came more quickly than asked. After praying, Cherry fired a flare. It malfunctioned and zigzagged crazily in the water around the rafts. The light attracted a huge swarm of fish. When barracudas closed in on the fish, some of them jumped into Rickenbacker's raft. Now they had food to tide them over.

Seeing this, Whittaker's attitude toward God began to soften. But they were still perishing from dehydration.

On the eighth evening, Bill Cherry prayed for water—and soon. He knew they couldn't last another day. At twilight a rainstorm arrived with plenty of water. They cupped it in their hands for immediate relief, then soaked their shirts with it. The precious water squeezed from their shirts partially filled the life jackets. Seeing this dramatic answer to Cherry's prayer, Whittaker wondered if he should pray too.

Ninth day. The sun was blazing. There was no relief.

Tenth day. When one of the men prayed that God would

kill him, Rickenbacker yelled, "Cut that out! Don't bother Him with whining! He answers *men's* prayers!" Then Rickenbacker prayed that the Lord would rescue them and bring them to land.

Eleventh day. A welcome rain enabled the men to drink some of it, then save as much as possible. But the rainstorm upset Sergeant Kaczmarczyk's raft. When his friends pulled him out of the water, they knew he was dying. He died the next night. The other men, in a solemn and respectful service, committed his body to the deep.

Thirteenth day. Disappointment. A rainstorm was heading toward them, then reversed its course. This time it was Whittaker who prayed. He dared to ask God to send the rain back to them. God did, much to the amazement of the others—and of Whittaker himself.

Fourteenth day. The wind died down. The men were developing serious sunburns, blisters, and ulcers. Their clothing and their fishing lines were rotting. Rickenbacker asked God to save them from the doldrums, but no answer came.

On the eighteenth and nineteenth days, they spotted a search plane about three miles away, but the searchers didn't see them. It returned twice but still missed them. Whittaker did not despair. He believed that God would save them.

Twentieth day. They rowed the rafts away from one another so that the search plane would be more apt to see them. A plane came—but missed them.

On the morning of the twenty-first day, DeAngelis awakened Whittaker with the news that he saw palm trees on the horizon. When Whittaker looked, he confirmed that it was not a mirage. Neither DeAngelis nor Reynolds had the strength to do anything, but Whittaker was miraculously empowered to row for seven and a half-hours.

When they were 250 yards from shore, a strong current swept them a mile out from land. Sharks threatened to upset the raft, and a reef imperiled them. But they finally reached shore and were met by friendly natives. Their hosts showed them every kindness and notified the U.S. Navy. When the Navy finally reached them, they learned that Bill Cherry, Rickenbacker, and the others had been rescued.

A recovered Whittaker returned to the States to tell his story of a recovered faith.

JUST THE RIGHT WORD

For several months Evelyn Johnson had been experiencing muscle weakness and hoarseness. Preliminary tests gave no indication of serious trouble. She seemed to be in good health. It was not until a neurologist entered the case that tests indicated a major problem.

In December 1994, Evelyn and her husband Milt had an appointment with the neurologist. It was then he broke the shattering news that she had Lou Gehrig's disease (amyotrophic lateral sclerosis or ALS). There was no known cause and no known cure. It was a death sentence.

From the human point of view the situation was hopeless. But Evelyn and Milt were strong Christians. Their roots were deep in God. The words of Psalm 1:3 fitted them well. They were like a tree planted by rivers of water, that brings forth its fruit in its season. Its leaf doesn't wither and whatever the person does will prosper. Evelyn had had years of rich experience teaching ladies' Bible classes. She and Milt had touched many lives for God. They had raised a family for the Lord. They were model believers. Now how would they react?

In the car they wept briefly, then made a covenant that they would not give way to despair or discouragement.

They were in a win-win situation. To live would be Christ. To die would be gain.

On the way home, Evelyn remembered that she wanted to buy a gift for a Christian friend at a neighborhood department store. At the store, a Salvation Army bell ringer was passing out little cards to donors entering. It was the first time the Johnsons had ever seen the Salvation Army giving cards to donors. As Evelyn passed, she received a card with the following message:

> *But thanks be to God! He gives us the victory through our Lord Jesus Christ* (1 Cor. 15:57). Thank You, Father, for giving me the desire to keep going when it feels as if my problems will crush me.

These words of encouragement spoke powerfully to two troubled hearts. The Johnsons knew that the Lord had sent that message especially for them at that precise moment.

In the days that followed, Evelyn's condition declined steadily. As family and friends showered her with love, she continued to minister to them by the example of her life and by her words of wisdom. When she could no longer climb the stairs, Milt installed an electric chair lift. Then a wheel chair was necessary.

Finally Evelyn moved from home to a hospice. As breathing became more difficult, the doctor wanted to perform a tracheotomy, but she said *no*. She preferred to go home to heaven. On her last night some young Christian friends joined Milt and the family at the bedside and sang some old, familiar hymns. It was with such a musical background that Evelyn joined the heavenly choir, singing the praises of the Lord she loved. As she took her last breath, Milt said quietly, *"Absent from the body...at home with the Lord"* (2 Cor. 5:8).

THE CROSS IS THE ANSWER

Aleksandr Solzhenitsyn became known in the Soviet Union for his moral courage in confronting the authoritarian regime and in enduring oppression. He spent years in labor camps where conditions were unspeakable. Many inmates died from starvation, disease, and torture. Others gave up and committed suicide. Solzhenitsyn felt he too had reached his limit. He could see nothing more hopeful than to take his own life. He put down his shovel and sat down on a nearby bench. If a guard saw him loafing, he would probably kill him with the shovel. At this critical juncture, a wrinkled old man he had never seen in the gulag came and sat beside him. Bending forward, the man picked up a small stick and drew a cross on the dirt floor. Not a word was spoken. None was necessary. The stranger left. Solzhenitsyn realized in a flash that the Cross was the answer. Alone he could do nothing, but through the Cross he could find power and freedom. It was the Cross that gave him the strength to go on. It gave meaning to life.

> The cross! It takes our guilt away;
> It holds the fainting spirit up;
> It cheers with hope the gloomy day,
> And sweetens every bitter cup.
> —*T. Kelly*

He picked up the shovel and went back to work.

The day had begun with no promise of anything momentous. But then a stranger, a stick, and a Cross scratched in the dirt. These were the instruments in God's hand to give hope to Aleksandr Solzhenitsyn and to use him as a modern-day prophet.

In 1970 he won the Nobel Prize for literature, and came to the West four years later. A man of Christian principles, he did not find a sympathetic audience in the United States. He felt that the people were complacent in their wealth and unwilling to face harsh realities. When he delivered the commencement address at Harvard in 1978, he spoke out against the abuse of freedom, compromise with evil, and addiction to comfort. The audience booed. After 20 years in exile, he returned to Russia in 1994.

RUTHIE'S REMARKABLE REQUEST[9]

One night when Helen Roseveare was working in the labor ward of a mission hospital, a patient died after giving birth to a premature baby. She also left a two-year-old daughter. To keep the baby alive, the staff went into full alert. One wrapped the infant in cotton wool; another brought a box to be used as a bassinet. When a third tried to fill the only hot water bottle, it burst (rubber has a short life in the tropics). Alternative methods went into high gear.

The next day, at prayer time, Helen shared the need with some of the orphan girls. It was then that a ten-year-old named Ruthie prayed: "Please, God, send us a hot water bottle. It'll be no good tomorrow. The baby will be dead, so please send it this afternoon." Then, as an afterthought, she added: "And while You are at it, would You please send a dolly for the little sister, so she'll know You really love her."

At moments like this, older Christians often fear that such childlike prayers are too audacious, and that when they are not answered, tender faith will be shattered. Up to this time no one had ever sent Miss Roseveare a parcel from home (the U.K.), and even if they had, "common sense" would tell them not to send a hot water bottle to the equator.

In mid-afternoon, Helen received word that a car had

arrived at her home with a 20-pound parcel. She raced across the yard with the orphan girls following and ripped away the wrapping. As 40 youngsters watched breathlessly, she lifted out clothes, bandages, soap, a box of raisins. Then as she reached in again, she grasped a rubber hot water bottle. She wept. She hadn't dared to ask God to send it, and didn't believe that He would.

At that moment, Ruthie pushed forward and said, "If God has sent the bottle, He must have sent the dolly too." Reaching down into the box, she pulled out a beautiful new doll and asked, "Can I go over with you, Mommy, and give this dolly to that little girl, so she'll know that Jesus really loves her?" Five months before this, a Christian girls' class in Britain had packed the box, including the unlikely hot water bottle and a doll contributed by one of the girls.

Ruthie had prayed for the bottle and the doll to arrive "this afternoon." It did. God had set the wheels in motion twenty weeks earlier.

THE TREASURED NEW TESTAMENT

During the Vietnam War, the Viet Cong overran Laos and captured two young missionaries, Sam Mattix and Lloyd Oppel, forcing them to march approximately 500 miles along the Ho Chi Minh trail to Hanoi in North Vietnam. The trip took 40 days. Mattix and Oppel were imprisoned in what was cynically called the Hanoi Hilton, actually a place of torture and brutality. Most of the inmates were U.S. prisoners of war, both officers and enlisted.

The two missionaries were probably suspected of being government agents. Food was minimal, sanitation intolerable, and reading matter scarce. Lloyd, Sam, and two other Christians tried to reconstruct as much of the Scriptures as they could remember, but they felt it was pitifully little. Later, in response to repeated requests, a guard brought a Gideon New Testament to them. This little book became so much in demand that its use had to be rationed. A man could have it only 30 minutes before slipping it to the next person on the list. Even hardened, cursing military men who in better circumstances would have nothing to do with Christianity found themselves reading God's Word.

Finally the war was over, and what seemed like age-long detention was ended. It was time for the men to go home. One day the men were ordered to assemble in the prison yard for inspection of zipper bags that had been issued to them to hold their personal items. When a guard checked the contents of Lloyd's bag and found the New Testament, he barked, "Why are you trying to take it? I told you that it belongs to the prison." The guard set the Testament on the inspection table.

When the senior officer, who professed to be an atheist and was at the same time a southern gentleman, saw what had happened, he strolled by the table, surreptitiously slid the book off in the palm of his hand, and stashed it in his bag. It was not until the men were flying to Clark Air Force Base in the Philippines on the first segment of their journey home that this senior officer came down the aisle to where Lloyd was sitting and said, "There's something I have for you." As cameras flashed, he handed him the priceless New Testament. Inside, the officer had signed his name and added, "Complimentary Issue." It was a tender word of assurance and encouragement from a Father who cares for His faithful servants.

We won't know the rest of the story until we get to heaven. Were men converted to God as they read the New Testament in the prison? And what about that senior officer? Did he ever repent and believe in the Savior?

THE BLACK MAMBA

The black mamba is the most dangerous and most feared snake in Africa. Mambas range in length from 70 to 140 inches and can travel at about nine miles an hour. They pack a large reserve of venom and inject a lethal dose at a single bite. The body absorbs the poison rapidly, causing paralysis of the breathing system.

Virginia Ross was distracted from her missionary work when she heard her baby daughter Jean crying on the veranda of their Zambian house. Virginia plucked the one-year-old out of the playpen, but found that ants had bitten her. After changing her and caring for the bites, the mother started back to the veranda. As she approached the playpen, a black mamba came out of it, straight toward them. The front third of its body was in the air, the rest providing the locomotion. Virginia remembers breathing a quick prayer for protection.

Mambas are most dangerous when someone or something blocks the way to their lair. Obviously this was so on the veranda. The snake, however, suddenly changed course and darted unseen into an old, unused stove that was nearby.

Virginia called to her husband, Archie, who was down a hill, engaged in what they say is one of a missionary's main occupations: fixing his car. Archie searched for the mamba without success so went back to the car.

Later, an African houseboy who was doing some ironing on the porch saw the snake, let out a shrill scream, and then leaped to the ground. When Archie came back, he decided to force the mamba out by lighting a fire in the stove. The snake emerged, curling itself in coils, all 9 feet of them.

Armed with a rake, Archie was able to pin it down, then dispatch it quickly.

Questions. Had the snake been in the playpen when the baby was there? How did ants happen to bite little Jean at that particular moment, summoning the mother? Why did the mamba change course when it could have struck Virginia? Coincidences? I don't think so.

FAITH RECOVERED[10]

The U.S.–Vietnam War was raging. Hien was a young Christian from South Vietnam. Because he was proficient in English, the American army employed him as an interpreter. But the Vietcong had him under surveillance through their undercover agents. Eventually they closed in on him, arrested him, and threw him into prison.

Then began an intensive program of brain washing. Day after day he was subjected to mental torture. The writings of Marx and Engel were drilled into his brain. Finally he broke under the pressure. He disavowed God. He could not believe in Him anymore.

His temporary assignment at that time was to clean the latrines. The stench was overpowering. One day at work he resolved not to pray any more. What was the use? The next morning as he was emptying a wastebasket, he noticed a piece of paper. As soon as he had washed the dirt from it, he saw "Romans 8" in the upper right-hand corner. Then he read:

And we know that all things work together for good to those who love God, to those who are called according to His purpose...What shall we say then to these things? If God is for us, who can be against us?...Who is he that condemns?...Who shall separate us from the love of Christ? Shall tribulation, or distress, or persecution, or famine, or nakedness, or peril, or sword?...In all these things we are more than conquerors, through Him who loved us.

It was as if Niagara had burst from his eyes. His tears flowed. The next day he went to the commandant and asked permission to clean the latrines every day. It was a bizarre request, but the commandant granted it. That same commandant had a copy of the New Testament, but, atheistic Communist that he was, he was using it as toilet tissue. Every day Hien retrieved a page of the New Testament, cleaned off the human excrement, washed it, and took it back to his bunk. When the other prisoners were asleep, he lay under the mosquito net and read the Sacred Word.

In the meantime he became part of a team that was planning to escape. The Vietcong got wind of the plot and hauled him in for interrogation.

"You are trying to escape. Aren't you?"

He answered "No."

"Tell us the truth. You are trying to escape."

Again he lied.

Then his conscience smote him. He had failed the Lord by lying. He determined that if the soldiers asked him again, he would tell the truth.

They came back a third time. "You're trying to leave the country. Aren't you?"

This time he answered "Yes."

They took him to a room in the prison, ostensibly to punish him. But he was amazed to hear them say, "We want to go with you."

As secretly as possible they commandeered a boat and took off for Thailand. It was a rough voyage. They were sure they would have drowned if the soldiers had not been able seamen. In the goodness of God they reached Thailand at last—and a new life.

Today Hien has a business degree and is carrying on a ministry for the Lord in California.

LOST CONTACT

To be perfectly honest, Brenda was plenty scared when she started to climb a rock cliff with some Christian friends. But she had committed herself to do it so there was no turning back. The cliff seemed almost perpendicular as she moved up the face of it. She was holding the rope as if her life depended on it—and it did.

It was a relief when she got to a ledge where she could take a breather. Apparently the person at the top of the cliff snapped the rope by mistake. The rope hit one of Brenda's eyes and knocked out the contact lens. Talk about a hopeless situation. The lens is small and transparent, and Brenda was on the side of a granite promontory. With both hands glued to the rope, she searched the ledge on which she was standing, but even if it were there, she wouldn't be able to see it because her vision was blurry. She was far from home where she had a duplicate set. Even at ground level there would be no place where she could replace it. In her desperation she shot up a prayer to the Lord. After all, He is the God of the impossible, isn't He? Yes, that's true, but isn't this stretching things a little? Isn't this asking too much?

As she struggled to the top of the cliff, she still hoped that one of the girls there might be able to find the lens in the corner of Brenda's eye. Unfortunately this did not happen. The lens was not there. There was nothing to do but wait for the rest of the party to reach the top, then start out for home. She looked at the magnificent range of mountains and thought of 2 Chronicles 16:9: *"For the eyes of the Lord run to and fro throughout the whole earth...."* Then she prayed, "Lord, you can see all these mountains. You know every single stone and leaf that's on them, and You know exactly where my contact lens is."

When the whole group had reached the top, they took the trail and hiked to the bottom. No sooner were they there than they heard a voice from the cliff, "Hey, you guys! Anyone lose a contact lens." It was from some hikers who had just started up the face of the cliff. Brenda and her friends hurried to the girl who had shouted. She explained that as she was climbing, she saw an ant carrying the lens slowly across the face of the rock. If it were not for the movement of the ant, she would never have seen it. But why would an ant want a lens?

Brenda's father is a cartoonist. When she told him about this remarkable story, he drew a picture of the ant lugging the contact lens across the wall of the cliff. A line leads from the ant to a balloon-shaped cloud with the words, "Lord. I don't know why You want me to carry this thing. I can't eat it and it's awfully heavy. But if this is what You want me to do, I'll carry it for You."[11]

THE ANGEL DOG

Julie and her daughter Tiffany had decided to take a vacation in France. Instead of going on an organized tour, however, they chose to do it alone—just the two of them. They felt they would have more freedom to "explore" and to travel at their own speed.

One of the cities on their itinerary was Carcassonne in the south. After checking in at their hotel in the late afternoon, they decided to go out sightseeing. They climbed to the top of the city wall, where they had an impressive view, but as they circled the city, they realized that they had become disoriented. They had no idea how to get back to the hotel. It was scary to be lost in a strange country where the people spoke a strange language and where darkness was descending.

As they walked along the wall, a German shepherd dog befriended them. He acted as if he had always known them, as if he was a family member. Julie was a bit wary and urged him to leave. He did leave briefly but must have had second thoughts so came right back and tagged along with them.

When they descended to street level, they saw a passage-way that Julie was sure would take them to the hotel. But it was dark and eerie, and she was nervous. The dog was not nervous. He seemed to want to escort them down the alley, so they followed him. When they came to a brightly-lit street, they could see their hotel. The dog turned around and left them, as if he knew his mission was accomplished.

Julie and Tiffany named their friend "the angel dog." Who can doubt he played the role of a guardian angel, even if dogs are never called angels?

MY FRIEND BRAD

Dick was waiting in the hospital Father's Room while his wife, Betty, was giving birth to their second child. When the chaplain finally arrived, the news was not good. The doctors were having a hard time getting the baby to breathe; x-rays showed that several organs were out of place; and the lungs had collapsed. The chaplain wanted permission to baptize the baby, but Dick could see no scriptural justification for infant baptism and he wasn't in a mood to engage in a theological discussion. Eventually, however, he did consent to an autopsy.

On the way home at 2 A.M., he stopped by to tell Betty's parents, who were on furlough from the Chad Republic. As

Dick rehearsed the story about little Brad's death, Mr. Rogers said that they had lost a son, John, the same way.

Just then the phone rang. It was the chaplain, saying, "Sanders, it's just like you said. If God wanted him alive, he'd be alive, or if He wanted to take him, He would. But he's alive." In his emotional exhaustion, Dick was unbelieving. After all, he had signed autopsy papers for Brad. Was the chaplain out of his mind?

Dad Rogers persuaded Dick to go back to the hospital and investigate, just in case the report was true. Sure enough, a nurse had insisted on giving the baby mouth to mouth resuscitation. She would not stop. Finally little Brad began to breathe. But there was still the problem of the misplaced organs. The hospital called a specialist but he wasn't at home. Actually he was right there at the hospital, working on another patient. When he aspirated some fluid and Brad's lungs filled with air, the other organs moved into their normal position.

During all this time, however, there had been a lack of oxygen reaching Brad's brain. As he grew, Betty and Dick noticed that he didn't move any of his limbs like other babies. A visit to a clinic revealed that he did indeed have a severe case of cerebral palsy. Betty learned of a procedure known as patterning by which the arms and legs are flexed rhythmically, as in a crawl, in an effort to teach the brain to activate the limbs, but it didn't work in Brad's case after three-and-a-half years of trying.

In spite of the well-meaning advice of friends, there was never a thought of entrusting Brad to anyone else's care. He was a *special* member of the family. His presence enriched their lives and taught them lessons they would never have otherwise learned.

Dick and Betty carried a full load of ministries at their home assembly in addition to their responsibilities at home until the summer of 1965 when God called them to serve him in the Chad. Again they never suffered from any lack of negative advice, but they simply did not believe that God would give them a little one as a reason for not going to the mission field.

With the passing of time, it became clear that Brad's mind was not impaired. The first clue came when Dick would imitate the sound of a plane and Brad's eyes would look up. The parents seized on this and did all they could to develop his mind, even if he could not speak. Both parents and brothers, Steve and Nate, developed a unique communication system with Brad; they learned to interpret the movement of his eyes.

Dick and Betty served on the mission field for 14 years, then returned to the ministry at their home assembly in Illinois. They started a company known as Brad's Toys, making playthings and equipment for disabled persons.

In 1988 Brad was able to communicate to his parents that he had trusted the Lord Jesus as his only hope for heaven. There was no doubt as to his sincerity. Accordingly it was arranged for him to be baptized. Dick and two other men lifted him and then lowered him into the tank. Dick says, "At that point I lost it." He was overcome emotionally.

From the time he first turned on a computer, Brad seemed to know what he was doing. He taught himself to use it by moving a track ball mounted in front of his chin. Later with a headband holding an infrared device, Brad could direct the light ray onto the monitor and activate commands. Soon he was sufficiently proficient to work as a draftsman, designing second floor additions for ranch houses, modified chairs, ramps, eating devices for disabled people, and even houses. He drew up plans for a hitch on his power chair so he could give children rides in his trailer and help his father by transporting materials to the carpenter shop. The power chair now pulls a snowplow and a snow thrower.

His most recent breakthrough is his ability to speak by means of new computer technology. Brad points the infrared ray to letters, words, and pre-programmed phrases which he often uses. They are then translated into a mechanical voice through a box at his side. He demonstrated his proficiency with this innovation at a convention in California.

Brad's favorite verse is John 9:3. When the disciples asked why a certain blind man was born blind, Jesus answered, *"Neither this man nor his parents sinned, but **that the works of God might be revealed in him"** (emphasis added). Brad's passion is to be used to glorify God. His challenge to others is not to wait until you're *perfect* to serve Him, but let God use you right now, as you are. This has been true in his life. God has used him and his disability. On a flight to the Chad in 1971, a young French Christian sat behind the Sanders, watching them intently. At this time he had given up hope of serving the Lord because he felt his wife could not tolerate the climate in Africa. He had joined the military instead. But after watching Brad and his brothers interacting on the plane, he went back to France and brought his wife out to the mission field. Christ had spoken to him through Brad without a word on Brad's part.

PART III

GOD'S WONDERFUL REDEMPTION

We are God's very own,
being redeemed by Him.
Every Christian therefore
should wear a sign on his heart,
"Not for sale!"

ANONYMOUS

GOD'S WONDERFUL REDEMPTION[1]

What a wonderful redemption!
Never can a mortal know
How my sin, though red like crimson,
Can be whiter than the snow.
—*Thoro Harris*

God is wonderful in creation. He is wonderful in providence. And He is wonderful in redemption. The great Creator and Provider is also the Savior.

In all His works behold Him great,
Before, almighty to create,
Almighty now to save.
—*T. Kelly*

Spurgeon said, "Creation and providence are but the whisper of His power, but redemption is its music, and praise is the echo which shall yet fill His temple." In the stories that follow, we hear the music of His power, and we respond with praise to our Great Redeemer.

WHERE SIN ABOUNDED[2]

Miguel[3] was a swashbuckling, rum-drinking, partygoer

with alley-cat morals. Yet when he rode around town, people respected him as a shrewd and moneyed businessman. He came from a family that owned property and cattle; they were more financially comfortable than their peasant neighbors. They belonged to the church that dominated the town and therefore assumed they were Christians. They had been taught that they should not read the Bible and should avoid people who did.

Miguel never missed a religious or national celebration, which usually turned into all-night partying. As the rum flowed freely, the music got louder and the dances more indecent. Drunkenness led to arguments, fights, and an occasional homicide.

It was at one of these parties that Miguel met an attractive young lady whom I will call Maria. As inconspicuously as possible, they stole away from the party to spend the night in a seedy hotel.

In the morning loud pounding on the door awakened them. It was their emotionally distraught parents, loudly decrying the shame this couple had brought on both family names. There was only one thing to do. Miguel and Maria must go to the Justice of the Peace and get married. When the brief ceremony ended, the two families parted. Miguel never saw his wife again. He contented himself that a quick divorce would solve the problem, but somehow he never got around to arranging it. Instead he built a house, took a mistress, and began a family.

Now he had land, cattle, a house, money, and a family—everything but satisfaction. So he built another house and took another mistress. During this time he never missed an all-night party.

Thinking it would give him even more status in the rural community, he built a third house, and took a third mistress. A prosperous farm, three houses, three common-law wives, plenty of children—yet he was still not satisfied.

One time, after a night of drunken carousing, he was riding home, trying to steady himself in the saddle. As he came down the mountainside, he heard people singing in one of the houses. It could only be the despised evangelicals. They were the only ones who sang together like that. Drawing nearer, he could tell they were singing about Jesus.

He decided to disrupt the gathering, so with a wild shout, he drove the horse through the door of the thatch-roofed, one-room house. The singing stopped, but instead of the brawl that he expected, he was greeted graciously and kindly. One man invited him to sit down with them and suggested that one of the young fellows would tether the horse outside.

Utterly embarrassed and confused, Miguel turned the horse around and left for home. He had a sleepless night. Never had he met people like that. They were different. They returned evil with kindness. They had shown not a trace of hostility or resentment.

The next morning he had no peace until he rode back and apologized for the disturbance he had caused. The family living there, just simple folks, invited him to sit down and have a cup of coffee with them. After assuring him he was forgiven, they told him how they had been born again through faith in the Lord Jesus and their great desire was to please Him in all things. When Miguel left, they gave him a New Testament.

Now 40 years old, Miguel began to read the Book that he had always been taught not to read or study. The Book seemed to grip him. He read it over and over until it seemed to be a part of him. And he kept visiting the family on the hill, learning from people who were, educationally and financially, much lower than he.

Finally it happened. He realized that the Bible is the Word of God. Alone in his home, he knelt, repented of his sinful, ungodly life, and acknowledged Jesus as his Lord and Savior.

Great rejoicing erupted among the evangelicals. They closed ranks with him, patiently teaching, encouraging, and counseling him. He was now their brother in Christ. Class distinctions had vanished.

But there was still Miguel's tangled marital life. He had a legal wife whom he had not seen since their marriage. If he divorced her, she could claim half of everything he owned. There were the three mistresses and the horde of children.

After much prayer, study of the Word, and consultation, he decided he should stay with the first and oldest of his common-law wives. By this time she had become a true believer. But he also covenanted to provide for the other two families as well. The details were worked out with remarkable harmony on all sides. Yet he still was not divorced from his legal wife so he could not be legally married to another.

One day on his way to town to meet with his lawyer, he met a messenger on the trail with a telegram. The news shocked him. His legal wife had just died.

That same day he and his companion rode down the mountainside to the little town to be married by the Justice of the Peace.

As he grew in grace and in the knowledge of the Lord Jesus, Miguel became a spiritual pillar in the assembly. Now widely known and respected as a godly Christian, he traveled extensively, telling forth the excellencies of the One who had called him out of darkness into His marvelous light. Many were saved and built up in the truth through his ministry.

God overruled his marital chaos in remarkable ways. The two mistresses from whom he separated after his conversion became believers and married Christians. A daughter of one of them became active in Christian service with her husband. Most of the children from the three families were eventually saved; some entered full-time service for the Lord.

Miguel never wavered in his spiritual convictions. He knew his Bible well, and loved to talk about the Lord. Over 80 when he died, he was strong in faith, giving glory to God.[2]

Dr. Livingstone, I Presume?[4]

Henry Martin Stanley is popularly remembered as the journalist who searched for David Livingstone in Africa, and who, when he finally saw the white face of the missionary, greeted him with those famous words, "Dr. Livingstone, I presume?"

Actually Stanley's birth name was John Rowlands. When his Welsh mother rejected him, he was shuttled between reluctant relatives until he finally landed in a poorhouse. He ran away when he was 15, only to spend more miserable time with his mother's relatives. This ended when he sailed as a cabin boy from Liverpool to New Orleans.

There this young Welshman met a wealthy merchant, Henry Morton Stanley, who adopted him, gave him his own name, and promised to take care of him financially. Although his benefactor died shortly afterward, young Henry's life now had a new direction. It was the first time he had ever felt loved and respected.

He subsequently served as a soldier, seaman, and journalist. In this latter role he met James Gordon Bennett of the *New York Herald*, who in 1869 commissioned him to "find Livingstone." The missionary's whereabouts in Africa had been virtually unknown for several years. On March 21, 1871, the well-known meeting took place.

"Dr. Livingstone, I presume?"

"Yes, sir."

"Dr. Livingstone, I am a press reporter, assigned to do a story on your life. But I want you to know two things about me. Number one, I am the biggest swaggering atheist on the face of the earth. Please don't try to convert me. Number two. Someone has sent some medicine for you."

"Please give me the medicine."

In time, as the two men went on safaris together, Stanley marveled at the life of David Livingstone.

Later he wrote:

I went to Africa as prejudiced against religion as the worst infidel in London. To a reporter like myself, who had only to deal with wars, mass meetings, and political gatherings, sentimental matters were quite out of my province. But there came to me a long time for reflection. I was out there away from a worldly world. I saw this solitary old man, David Livingstone, and I asked myself, "Why does he stay out here in such a place? What is it that inspires him?

For months after we met, I found myself listening to him, wondering at the old man carrying out the words, "Leave all to follow Me." But little by little, seeing his piety, his gentleness, his zeal, his earnestness, and how he went quietly about his business, I was converted by him, although he had not tried in any way to do it.

It was four months after their historic meeting that the biggest swaggering atheist on the face of the earth knelt down on African soil and gave his life to Jesus Christ. He said, "The power of that Christ-life was awesome, and I had to buckle in. I could not hold out any longer."

MONEY TALKS

One day a business colleague asked Cathie, "Are you one of those born againers?" She allowed that she was, but didn't really feel like pursuing the matter. She knew she should be "ready in season, out of season," but she wanted the Lord to make an exception that day. She just didn't want to witness to the man. She was distracted by her broken marriage and by her ex-husband's lawsuit to give him more time with the children.

Mac, however, wouldn't drop the subject. He was looking for something to fill the awful vacuum in his life. So he unknowingly kept giving her wonderful open doors that she could have entered with the gospel. But Cathie did not grab the opportunities. Finally she said to him, almost in exasperation, "Look, if you want to know God, why don't we tell Him?" They found a quiet place where they prayed together, asking the Lord to reveal Himself to Mac in an unmistakable way.

The next day Mac went into a bar and ordered a $3.50 beer. He paid for it with a five-dollar bill. As change the bartender gave him a dollar bill and two quarters. Before putting the bill in his wallet, he noticed that someone had written "John 20:29" on it.

That night he found a New Testament and looked for John 20:29. He was astonished to read, *"Thomas, because you have seen Me, you have believed. Blessed are those who have not seen and yet have believed."*

Mac knew that God had spoken. Those words were tailored just for him. The Lord had answered his prayer. He also knew that there was nothing for him to do but to trust the Savior. That is what he did. Alone in his bedroom, he bowed his head and said, "Father, the best way I know how, I receive Jesus Christ as my Savior. Cleanse me from my sins and make me the person you want me to be."

Then and there the great transaction was done. Mac went forth to serve the Lord who cared enough about him to use a defaced five-dollar bill to get his attention.

WHY?[5]

Glenn Chambers boarded his flight in New York, en route to Quito, Ecuador, to serve with Christian radio station HJCB, "the Voice of the Andes." No doubt his heart was filled with a sense of exhilaration and anticipation. After all, few things are as fulfilling as stepping out in service for the One who died for us on the cross of Calvary.

Glenn had to change planes at Miami, so he used the wait to write a note to his mother. He didn't have any stationery but used a folder with advertising on it. At the top of the first page was the single word "Why?" In the blank spaces, he scribbled out a short report of his flight so far.

He never did arrive in Quito. Not far from the airport, a mountain, El Tablazo, rises 14,000 feet into the sky. Chambers' plane crashed inexplicably into the mountain and the flaming wreckage tumbled into a ravine below. Of course, all on board were killed.

The news of his death reached his mother quickly and then a few days later she received the note he had mailed from the Miami airport. In big letters was the word "Why?" A good question. Why did he have to die so young, when he was so anxious to serve the Lord? Was this a victory to be chalked up to Satan's account? What good could possibly come out of such a tragedy? At the time the only comforting answer was found in the Savior's words, *"What I am doing you do not understand now, but you will know after this"* (Jn. 13:7).

Twenty-seven-and-a-half years later a valiant missionary

was scouting out unreached territory in the mountains of Ecuador. To her surprise she met a tribe of people who were bilingual. They could speak Spanish as well as their own tribal language. They seemed to be of unusual intelligence. Best of all, the chief and many of the people told her they were Christians.

How could they be Christians? To the best of her knowledge, no one had ever reached this far into the jungle with the gospel. When she asked them how they came to know the Lord Jesus as their Lord and Savior, the chief went into a hut and returned with a charred briefcase. Inside was a Spanish Bible. When the missionary opened to the flyleaf, she read, "Presented to our dear brother, D. Glenn Chambers." Christian friends on Long Island, New York Island signed it.

The chief explained that on a trip through the jungle they had found the briefcase and that through reading the Bible they had found the Lord. They had obviously been where Glenn Chambers' plane had crashed.

Glenn's life had not been wasted. Through his well-worn Bible the light of the gospel had streamed into the hearts of jungle people and made them new creatures in Christ Jesus.

TEX WATSON OF THE MANSON FAMILY[6]

The Manson Family was a gang of drug-crazed hippies who terrorized others with their mindless and vicious crimes. The leader, Charles Manson, exerted hypnotic power over his young female admirers, even to the point that they were glad to commit murder at a word from him. His hold over all members of the Family was "complete and wholly evil." The brutal murder of actress Susan Tate, age 26 and eight-and-a-half months pregnant, caused panic in Hollywood. No one knows how many murders the Family engineered; Manson boasted of 35. The story of their exploits does not make pleasant reading.

Tex Watson was one of the more than 40 "disciples." As a 23-year-old, he had left Copeville, Texas, for the glitz and glamor of Southern California. Before the trip ended he picked up a hitchhiker named Dennis Wilson. It was at Dennis's home that he met Charles Manson. He immediately charmed, even mesmerized, Tex. Incredible as it seems, he mistook Manson for Jesus Christ. His dedication was so great that he was willing not only to kill people but also to lay down his own life for the chief. Eventually he came to be one of Manson's main henchmen. Finally he was captured, tried, and convicted of seven counts of first-degree murder and of conspiracy. His death sentence was commuted to life imprisonment.

During six years of prison, Tex felt the Hound of Heaven pursuing him. His mother sent him a Bible, which he actually read at times. He heard a visitor witnessing about Christ to another inmate. Chaplains and others reached out to him with the gospel. He began to feel compassion for those whom he had killed, and guilt for the crimes he had committed. They were years of seeking to find peace.

During the last week of May 1975, a special series of meetings was held at the prison chapel. On the final night of the "revival," Tex decided that this had to be it.

I couldn't play games any longer. I understood very clearly what was being offered; God who made us, God from whom we'd turned away to follow our own selfishness, God who wanted us back as His sons and daughters, wanted *me* back. To bridge the gap between us, He'd sent His own Son to take our death—the inevitable consequence of our sin—on Himself. This had not only opened up an eternity of fellowship with our Creator in this life and the next; it made positive change and renewal possible in our lives right now, in *my* life right now. It began a process of slowly becoming the whole person one was born to be, of becoming more and more like Christ Himself. It wasn't just a fire escape—that actually had very little to do with it—it was letting ourselves be participants in a total victory over evil and death that was already won because Christ had risen from the dead. It was deciding that His Kingdom and His will for us were the only things that really mattered. Having decided to give Him our whole lives, we were to let the mighty Spirit of God come into our own spirits to start building the life of Christ in us, and to enable us to do the service to which we were called.

That is what it is all about, I thought as I sat in the back of the chapel on that last night, sensing that [the speaker] was reaching the end of his sermon. It occurred to me that to take this step would mean giving up even the most precious thing I had: the determination somehow to find the legal machinery that would get me out of prison and back into the world. It would mean, if that was God's will, accepting a natural life that never extended beyond the walls of the [prison] Colony; it would mean asking for nothing except to be used or even set aside for the glory of God. It would mean all that and more. When the invitation was given, I ran to the front.

Tex was baptized 15 days later in a large plastic laundry cart in the yard outside the chapel. He wrote:

No matter how silly it might have looked to someone from the outside, someone who didn't understand all that was going on at that moment, to me it was as glorious as the River Jordan where John [baptized] people in preparation for the coming of the Messiah. My Messiah had come, at last; He had come to me and I was His....That night, two weeks before when I'd stumbled forward in the chapel, I'd finally had a full realization of exactly what I had done, a realization so devastating, that all I had been able to do was weep for what seemed like hours. Now that burden was lifted; I would weep again, many times, for those I'd hurt—the dead and the living—but from now on it would be tears shed in the certainty that the punishment for that hurt had been taken and the debt paid—not by me, but by God Himself....For God the cost was immeasurable.

Tex is still in prison. Married and with four children, he carries on a pastoral ministry for the Lord Jesus in California Men's Colony.

God's grace to Tex Watson—and to us—is wonderful.

SAVED AND SURE OF IT

Milton Haack was 18 and tired of farm life in Minnesota. The outbreak of World War II gave him the chance to break away, so he enlisted in the Navy. The first day at Boot Camp was a cultural shock for him. He had come from a religious home. Milt had been baptized, confirmed, had become a member of the church, and had led a fairly decent life. With the rest of his family, he had faithfully observed the sacraments of the church. Now he was in a cesspool of cursing, filthy language, and obscene jokes. He consoled himself with the fact that if they all were killed in battle, at least he would have a good chance of getting into heaven.

From Boot Camp he was shipped to Boston, Massachusetts, prior to being assigned to a training school. One day in the barracks, he saw a sailor sitting on the edge of his bunk, reading a book. Milt was curious. It looked like a Bible but Milt knew it couldn't be. No one would have the courage to read the Bible in such an ungodly environment. Walking down the aisle between the rows of bunks, he peered through the corner of his eye. Sure enough, it was the Bible.

Milt spoke to the fellow, hoping to get into a theological argument with him. But the fellow took him off guard by telling him how he was converted to God. He knew that his sins were forgiven and that he was sure of heaven. Ridiculous. How could anyone know until he died and stood before God?

Finally Milt said, "Look, we've been arguing about salvation for 45 minutes and you haven't mentioned the most important requirement."

"What is that?"

"Baptism. The Bible teaches that you have to be baptized to be saved, and you haven't said a word about baptism."

The Christian sailor quietly handed his Bible to him and said, "Please show me where it says that in the Bible."

Poor Milt. He didn't know the difference between Genesis and Revelation. Frustrated, he dropped the Bible onto the bunk and said, "I have a priest in Minnesota who said so, and that's good enough for me."

That night Milt asked God to get him out of that barracks, the sooner the better. It wasn't big enough for both of them. The prayer seemed to be answered when he was sent to a PT training school in Rhode Island. Now he could breathe more freely. That guy was out of his life, hopefully forever.

On a weekend liberty, he made his way to a park near the training center. He noticed two girls passing out leaflets. When one of them approached him and handed him one, he realized right away that it was religious. She asked him, "Are you saved?" Gr-r-r-r, he had just got rid of someone like that. Now here it was again.

"Yes, I'm saved," he fibbed, then quickly changed the subject.

But she was not easily deterred. "I would like to hear how you were saved."

In desperation he parroted the testimony of the sailor he had just got rid of in Boston. She did not pursue the matter, but invited him to come to a local chapel Sunday evening where he would hear men tell how they were converted to God. He promised to go and was true to his promise. What impressed him was that four men told of a specific experience in their life when they repented of their sins, received Jesus Christ by faith as Lord and Savior, and knew they were saved. He said to himself, "If these men are right, then I am on my way to hell."

Milt began to read a pocket New Testament that had been given to him in Boot Camp. John's Gospel was easiest to understand, and one verse, 5:24, was of special interest.

Verily, verily, I say unto you, He that heareth My word and believeth on Him that sent Me, hath everlasting life, and shall not come into condemnation but is passed from death unto life (KJV).

Now the time had come for this troubled sailor to be shipped out to the Philippines where the real war was going on. As his PT boat anchored off the island of Samar, he asked himself, "If I die, where will I spend eternity?"

One day an announcement blared over the public address system, "Now hear this. Bible study in the Base Chapel this evening at 20:00." As if driven by an unseen force, Milt took the liberty boat ashore and went to the chapel. Only four or five showed up for the study. The fellow who spoke on Ephesians seemed to make special effort to explain the gospel clearly. At the close they invited Milt to come to a "little time of devotion" they had every morning after chow at 07:00.

In the morning devotions one fellow again told the way

of salvation so clearly that even a fool could understand it. Then they all knelt and prayed. When Milt was the only one left, he felt backed into a corner. What to do now? He still remembered a chorus they had sung the night before, so from the depths of his heart he said:

> Thank you, Lord, for saving my soul.
> Thank you, Lord, for making me whole.
> Thank you, Lord, for giving to me
> Thy great salvation so full, so free.

He really meant it. When he rose from his knees, he was a new man in Christ Jesus.

Word quickly spread among the crew of the PT boat that Haack had "got religion." It was predictable that his shipmates would begin to taunt him about his faith. One evening when Milt came topside on his way to the Bible study, he found the Skipper and the crew having a party. The beer was flowing freely. The Skipper called out, "Hey guys, hide your cans of beer; Reverend Haack is coming through." Everyone laughed.

Someone else called out, "Hey Haack, pray for us that we won't get too drunk tonight." Again more laughing.

Milt had had enough. Standing at the stern of the boat, he said, "Men, unless you repent of your sin and believe in the Lord Jesus Christ as your Savior, you are on your way to hell." Then as he disembarked, he called back, "And Skipper, that goes for you too." That was a bad move. In the Navy you don't talk like that to a superior officer, and especially to the Captain. Milt knew he was in trouble. Sure enough, when he returned from the Bible study, the man on watch said that the Captain wanted to see him at 08:00 the next day.

After a night without sleep, the young sailor stood before the Skipper and heard the ominous words, "I want to talk to you about what happened last night."

Milt replied, "Yes, sir, I understand."

The Skipper proceeded:

When I was 16, I went to a Christian summer camp and received the Lord as my Savior. For several years I was the happiest person in the world, but when I joined the Navy, something happened. You would never guess that I ever professed to be a Christian, would you? Well, I want to tell you I'm sorry for what I did to you last night. And I want to tell you that I am happy to have on my boat a Christian who is not afraid to stand up for Christ.

Then he added,

I've been looking over your records and I notice you've not had a promotion for a while. So I'm going to recommend you for a new rate. You will have another stripe in about a month.

Milt thanked him and left, humbly grateful that the Lord could use him in spite of his failures.

Now let's turn the calendar back to when Milt wrote to his parents about the change in his life. He waited anxiously for a reply, expressing their reaction. While his mother and dad did write to him, they never mentioned anything about his newfound faith. But when he went home after the war, the silence ended rather violently. His father said, "Either you give up this strange religion that says you can be sure of heaven or you get out of my house."

The returned veteran said, "I will go, but I take my Savior with me." Six years passed before he saw his parents again. They corresponded by mail but no mention of spiritual things was allowed. But a Christian couple in Minnesota kept up a friendship with the mom and dad, and 20 years after the separation, the parents were saved.

Again we turn the calendar back to the time that Milt

was stationed in Rhode Island. A romance began the day that Marjorie Simpson handed him a tract and asked him if he was saved. Milt and Marge were married when he returned from the war, and 12 years later they set out with their two children to serve the Lord as missionaries in the Philippines.

Milt was one of hundreds of men who went overseas in wartime in the service of their country and who subsequently returned in peacetime to serve the Captain of their salvation.

THE BIBLE PAGE WITH ONLY TWO WORDS

From boyhood Michael had heard Bible verses, both at home and in the local Christian fellowship. One verse that especially stood out was Romans 3:23, *"For all have sinned and fall short of the glory of God."* At no time would Michael have denied that he was a sinner. He was often mean to his friends. He selfishly wanted his own way. His thought life was impure. But there was no deep conviction of his sinfulness. He could live comfortably with it.

As a child, to win candy or other awards, he memorized a considerable number of Bible verses, sometimes a whole chapter, and in one instance the entire book of Philippians. The fact that hell is the eternal destiny of unsaved people began to eat away at him. He argued with God about it. Wasn't the punishment grossly out of proportion to the crime? How could a God of love treat him like that?

By the time he was 13, Michael knew all the right answers, so he told his parents that he believed, thinking that everything would be fine. This would get the monkey off his back. But it was a false profession. He hadn't really trusted Christ as his Lord and Savior. It was just a matter of words.

It was not until some years later that he was terrified by the realization that he really did deserve to go to hell. Added to that was the knowledge that Christ might return at any time, and Michael would not go to heaven with his saved family and friends. It was time to get desperate. So he took his Bible and asked God to lead him to the place he should read, the place where he would find the answer.

He opened the Bible. There he saw a page with only two words: New Testament. It was the page between the Old and New Testaments.

After a momentary disappointment, he concluded that God wanted him to read the New Testament. In the days ahead he read Matthew and Mark. By the time he reached Luke he realized that those who believe in Jesus will never be consigned to hell. It was the answer he was looking for.

By a simple act of faith, he confessed that he really was a sinner, that he believed Jesus died to pay the penalty of his sins, and that he received Christ as his only hope for heaven.

After that he experienced what he called "an incredible sense of relief." His sins were gone. His future was secure. He welcomed the prospect of the Savior's return.

We can only marvel at the ingenuity of God in leading Michael to the only page in the Bible with two words on it.

PILIASKI

The most remarkable thing about Piliaski was his size; he was only 4 feet 8 inches tall. As this young Zambian saw neighbors return from the Copper Belt, loaded with material possessions they had earned there, he decided that he too would go to the Copper Belt, get a job, buy a bicycle, a watch, blankets, and good clothing. He felt that as long as he lived in the bush, there was no future for him.

His first job was at a mine. Because he was dependable and a hard worker, he was put in charge of a squad of men. After a month, he had more money than he had ever seen before. But what to buy with it?

He went to the nearby town of Kitwe and did a lot of window-shopping. One store that impressed him sold books. In the window he saw a New Testament in his own language. He went inside and said to the clerk, "There's a book in your window that speaks to me."

"O then, you must be a Mumemba. That is the Bemba New Testament. Let me get one for you. It costs only three shillings."

Piliaski quickly bought the book, the first one he had ever owned, and triumphantly carried it back to his hut at the mining camp. There he had electricity for the first time in his life, so he was able to read the Testament every night after work hours. The story gripped him. He couldn't read enough. Soon the message revealed his own heart to him. He realized that, in God's sight, he was a guilty sinner and therefore unfit for heaven. He could endure it no longer. He asked the Lord to forgive him for being such a sinner and for having rebelled against His will.

Now he had Jesus as his Lord and Savior and Friend. Little Piliaski talked to Christ as his best Friend.

One night after reading the New Testament for an hour or so, he put out the light and meditated on what he had been reading. Then he was conscious of the Lord's presence in the room.

"Piliaski!"

"Yes, Lord."

"I want you to go back to your people and tell them about Me."

The little man obeyed and became an outstanding gospel preacher. Many were saved. But then Piliaski read in the

Word that believers should be baptized by immersion. He had never been baptized, so how could he tell his converts to follow the Lord in this way? He gathered all the believers at the river, and told the first convert to baptize him, and then he would baptize the others. With this company of baptized believers, an assembly began.

Years later, when the Bush wars broke out, the terrorists rounded up religious leaders and told them they were going to preach their last sermon. Some were too scared to speak. One collapsed. But Piliaski rose to the occasion. He said,

> Since this is going to be my last sermon, I am going to preach from my heart to your hearts. I know where I'm going and you need to know where you are going, so I will be preaching about heaven and hell." As he went on fearlessly, some of the armed men actually began to tremble. They said, "Look, get out of here. Get out of the village and this area, and don't ever come back.

Piliaski was the only one set free. As of this writing he is still preaching the gospel and still planting new assemblies.

He is a small man, but he casts a big shadow.

THE SEARCH FOR REST[7]

As a kid in Germany, Alois was happy and optimistic, yet he was driven by feelings of restlessness. The open road beckoned him with its promise of satisfaction and fulfillment. The pot of gold at the end of the rainbow was calling.

His passion for reading opened up vistas of grandeur in the outside world. This made his village life seem boring and colorless. Others might think it charming; for him it was Dullsville.

Alois's parents sent him to a parochial boarding school. Maybe this would provide some measure of satisfaction.

But his dreams were unfulfilled. All the time his spirit was saying, "Don't fence me in."

In public high school at age 17, he sat in a biology class and said to himself, "What am I doing, sitting here? Why am I not out in the world of reality where people live, love, suffer, and struggle? All they do here is lecture and theorize. I don't want only to think about life. I want to taste it."

Before the end of the school year, he stuffed his backpack and hitchhiked to France and Spain; he was the great adventurer, hippie, tramp. But his travels were short-lived. When he tried to go to Holland, he was stopped at the border as a missing person and shipped back to his parents. What a blow to his dreams. He went back to school, a tremendous waste of time.

Next he decided to try the rock-scene, which meant "Live fast. Love hard. Die young." But now the Army was calling him for military service. To avoid that horror, he would enter the seminary and become a priest. During the second semester he got a cheap flight to San Francisco and lived with other hippies in the Haight-Ashbury district. But their meaningless and senseless lives turned him off, so he flew back to the seminary, determined to spend his life serving others.

It didn't last. The restlessness returned, so he hitchhiked to Amsterdam where he earned money doing odd jobs and begging as a sidewalk musician. With that money he flew to New York where his cash was stolen right after his arrival. Nothing to do but hitchhike across the country to California. He stayed there until his visitor's visa expired, then he moved south to Mexico.

In Mexico, he frequented a fruit juice stand. There he met two girls, Laura and Tammy, who were different. They radiated an inner harmony, although they were relatively uneducated. When he asked them why they were different, they replied simply that they were Christians. When he tried to argue with them about Christianity, they would only say, "We believe in Jesus Christ. To Him we have confessed our sins and surrendered our lives. The Savior paid the penalty of our sins on the Cross, and now we have peace with God."

As time went on, Alois began to read the New Testament, which resulted in a deepening consciousness of his sinful condition before God.

By then he was working with the girls at the fruit juice stand, and he attended meetings of Christian young people with them.

One day he promised the girls he would not go with Don Lorenzo and participate in a sacred mushroom ceremony with a shaman. But he did, and when the girls found out about it, he was exposed as a liar. He was filled with shame and confusion. He had disappointed those he loved most.

The shame became intolerable. Finally he broke. He brought the load of his sin to the crucified Christ. Light dawned into his darkened heart. For 20 wasted years he had looked for satisfaction; now he found it in the Savior. He wept over the years he had lived without God. He wept with joy that his sins were now forgiven. He had found meaning, satisfaction, and fulfillment in the Lord Jesus. The rest he had sought in the world, he now found in his Redeemer. The God-shaped vacuum in his heart was filled.

Alois is still traveling, not as a hippie but as an ambassador of Jesus Christ. Proficient in eight languages, he tells forth the good news of free salvation through faith in the Savior of sinners.

ADONIRAM JUDSON, MISSIONARY TO BURMA[8]

Some New Englanders may have thought that young

Adoniram Judson was too clever for his own good. Other more charitable souls were impressed to see a 12-year-old teaching from the Book of Revelation to an adult Bible class from the original Greek. Still others were intimidated by his brilliance.

By the time he reached college, he considered himself wiser than God. His Christian classmates were afraid to debate him; they might lose what faith they had. His father warily tried to reason with him. His mother prayed for him.

His roommate, Jacob Eames, came to college professing to be a Christian, but under Judson's influence, he became a blatant atheist. Adoniram had won him over.

Years later Judson went to New York to be interviewed for theater work. On the long ride back to Boston, he pulled in to a hotel for a good night's rest. The manager was sorry; all the rooms were occupied. Judson was exhausted. He offered to pay the room price if he could sleep in the lobby and clear out before the other guests arose.

Then the manager mentioned that he did have a vacancy, but it was next to a room where the occupant was extremely ill. The dying man's crying, cursing, and convulsions would not be conducive to sleep. Judson, however, was so exhausted he was sure the noise from next door wouldn't bother him.

He was wrong. He lay awake, twisting and turning, listening to the cries of pain. Finally the noise stopped and Judson fell asleep.

When he was checking out in the morning, he asked about the sick man and learned he had died in the early hours of the morning.

Judson thought it was odd that a man should die in a hotel like that, so he quizzed the manager about the guest. The manager said, "It does seem strange. I've tried to contact his next of kin, but he died alone—a man of intelligence and status. He was an honors graduate from Providence College in Rhode Island. Name was Jacob Eames."

"What did you say his name was?"

"His name was Jacob Eames."

Judson later said,

When I started the trip back home, I couldn't see through my tears. Two words were pounding into my heart: death, hell, death, hell. I had to stop, get down in the dusty road and repent bitterly that I had betrayed my God and knocked out any faith that my friend Jacob Eames had in Him.

This experience changed the whole direction of Adoniram Judson's life. He went as a missionary to India, was expelled, and moved on to Burma. In his enthusiasm, he went up to a Burmese one day and gave him a great big hug. The man went home and told his family that he had seen an angel. Joy so characterized Judson's life that the people of Burma called him "Mr. Glory-Face."

Two wives in succession died. Three children died. Missionary colleagues died. Judson labored seven years before the first Burmese trusted Christ. Then so many turned to the Savior that he was thrown into prison by the authorities. After 18 months, he was put on a ship to return to the United States. He died en route. On his tombstone in Malden, Massachusetts, is an inscription: "The ocean is his sepulchre, the Burmese Bible is his monument. His record is on high."

Adoniram Judson had translated the Bible into Burmese. In Burmese folklore, there was a belief that some day a man was going to come with a book which would have the truth. Judson was the man, and the Burmese Bible was the book.

FROM THE GUTTER TO GOD[9]

On June 17, 1998, Germany's largest newspaper ran a one-page article on page 3 with a one-inch heading, "A Drug Addict in the Service of Jesus Christ." The sub-title was "Franz Huber: From the Gutter to God." The story was extraordinary for several reasons. It was about one of society's rejects. It was in a secular paper. It was sympathetic to Christianity.

Franz Huber was an illegitimate child, unwanted from his birth. His was a dysfunctional family. His biological father deserted, leaving him to a mother who had other interests (a live-in boyfriend whom he hated), and a grandmother who died when he was nine. He was a typical latchkey kid.

On his own at age 15, he started as a meat-cutter's apprentice, but that lasted only a year. Franz turned to marijuana to overcome rejection, loneliness, and the cruelties of life. That was the first step to 20 years of addiction to cocaine and heroin. The places where he slept were also home to prostitutes, pimps, criminals, addicts, and the cast-offs of society. He was in prison for four years, mostly for crimes committed to support his drug habit.

He and his girlfriend took LSD, smoked hash, opium, and morphine. If they couldn't get drugs, they went into the terrors of withdrawal. In a psycho ward, Franz was locked up with murderers, sex fiends, and lunatics. Life was insufferable.

Then the magnet pointed to Amsterdam. There he planned to take his last dose of heroin, the "golden shot" that would end it all. But a friend in the red-light district there told him about some Christians who had a house that ministered to addicts. Even though it would mean withdrawal (and Franz didn't want that), he knew that these

Christians were his last hope. He was drawn by love.

The Christians led him to the Lord. His life was totally changed. For one year he worked at the house, seeking to help other slaves to drugs.

When he finally returned to Munich, he worked in a pizza parlor, shoveled snow, and did other odd jobs. Most of the money he earned went to reimburse pharmacies from which he had stolen and to pay for property he had damaged.

With a Christian assembly in Munich as a base, Franz carried on a widespread Christian ministry to addicts and others in need. As the newspaper *Bild-Leitung* reported,

> His home became a place for all sorts of troubled people. Constantly Franz was trying to bring the Good News of the Gospel to the hopeless. He prayed with them, helped them, and his life was a testimony to God's grace.

He died of a brain hemorrhage on June 8, 1998. Three hundred people attended his funeral, most of them former drug addicts, punks, and tramps. It was their tribute to the man who had given them help, hope, and love.

O GOD, SAVE MY DADDY

Billy Stevenson was born in Northern Ireland when conflict between Protestants and Catholics was the ongoing news of the day. He had a Christian grandmother, a woman of prayer, but hers was the only spiritual influence in the home. Neither his father nor mother was a believer. That changed, however, when Billy was eight or nine; his mother was saved, then his father. From that time on the father read the Bible and prayed with the family every day. The Stevensons attended the meetings at the local Gospel Hall whenever the doors were open. Faithful Sunday School teachers planted a sacred deposit of God's Word in the lives of their pupils, and faithful preachers proclaimed the gospel so clearly that even a fool could understand.

Young Stevenson left school as soon as possible to take a job at a large engineering plant. He liked this contact with the outside world and began to adopt the lifestyle of his coworkers. Before long he was a heavy drinker, rebelling against God and trying to run from Him. There were the inevitable fights outside the tavern. Once he left some of his teeth on the sidewalk; at another time he suffered a fractured skull. Back at work, he always told the men what a great time he had had.

After abortive attempts to join the air force and navy, he signed up for duty with the army. His loving parents went to the pier to see him sail for London. As he was parting, his father said, "Son, you can't take from us the power and privilege of prayer. You leave behind a praying father and mother."

Life in London was a binge of booze and gambling. Eventually he was posted to Germany. There he wrote his girlfriend, asking her to marry him. She agreed, so he went back to Northern Ireland for the wedding, and then failed to return to Germany. The Royal Military Police finally found him lying drunk on a Belfast sidewalk. After arrest and imprisonment he was sent back to Germany for a tour of unwelcome menial duty. Then the army discharged him.

Back in Ireland, he had a wife but no job. Two children were born, a boy and girl. It wasn't much of a home, because Stevenson spent his money on liquor and horse racing.

The "troubles," as they were called, were escalating in Northern Ireland, and Billy joined the fray—on the Protestant side, of course. More than once he barely escaped gunfire and bombing.

After a drunken spree around Christmas 1970, he was taken to the hospital. There Mr. Jim Leckie came to visit him, and to talk to him about his need of salvation. Billy was not ready yet but Mr. Leckie was not easily discouraged. In the weeks that followed the hospitalization, he succeeded in getting the Stevensons to gospel meetings. After one of those meetings, Billy's wife said, "I'd like to be saved." And she was. As her husband later said, "She got what I wanted."

On April 18, 1971, Stevenson came home drunk. Mr. Leckie was there, waiting for him. Under Leckie's kindly persuasion, Billy went to hear Derek Bingham preach. The meeting is a blur in his mind. All he remembers is that the preacher said to him, "Don't wait."

At home with his wife and children, he felt that it was too late, that he had passed redemption point. Mrs. Stevenson suggested that he go upstairs and read John 14:1-6. As he passed the door of his son's room, he saw the little fellow on his knees by the bed and heard him pray, "God, save my drunken daddy. Don't let my daddy go to hell." When the lad heard his father's footsteps, he called out, "Daddy, I'm praying for you."

Billy rushed to his room, fell flat on the floor, and cried out to God, weeping, the words of the hymn:

> Jesus, I will trust Thee,
> Trust Thee with my soul;
> Guilty, lost, and helpless,
> Thou canst make me whole.
> There is none in heaven
> Or on earth like Thee:
> Thou hast died for sinners—
> Therefore, Lord, for me.

In that moment, Billy Stevenson, boozer, gambler, and

fighter became a new man in Christ. He hurried to embrace his wife and children and to tell them he had passed from death to life. He would be a new husband and a new daddy.

Three years later he went with his family as missionaries to Korea. And ever since then, wherever he travels he has been telling God's way of salvation to anyone who listens.

MARK PEASE FINDS PEACE

Mark came from an average Catholic home. His early life followed the usual pattern—baptized as an infant, confirmed, first Holy Communion, and parochial school—in his case up to grade seven. Yet his was a troubled childhood. He had to be harshly disciplined by the nuns. After he moved to public schools, his life was a downward spiral.

As soon as he was free from school, he decided to become an ironworker, climbing to dizzying heights on the steel skeletons of buildings under construction. It was dangerous work, even with a safety belt.

In his early 20s, Mark somehow renewed friendship with Joe, a fellow who professed to be a Christian. One night Joe explained the gospel to him, how Christ died for his sins, and all Mark had to do was receive Him as Lord and Savior. They prayed together, then Joe announced, "That's it. Now you're a Christian." But there was no repentance. They both continued in a sinful lifestyle.

On the evening of November 24 something extraordinary happened. Joe called and asked if Mark could come over and talk with him. It was extremely important, he said. When Mark reached the house, Joe was obviously agitated. Mark had never seen him so worried. He who professed to be a Christian blurted out the reason for his deep concern. He said that if either of them died without repenting and trusting Christ, they would both go to hell. The whole scene was eerie. Why was Joe in such a dither? Up to now, Mark had no thought of dying. But Joe's message hit him hard. Suddenly he was afraid to die. He worried all the way home. In the safety of his own house, the fear subsided, at least temporarily.

The reason for this upsetting incident became clear the next day. Mark was working on a steel framework 35 feet off the ground. In order to move along a catwalk, he had to disengage his safety belt. During that brief moment he lost his footing and fell to the ground with nothing to break his fall. Soon he realized he had no feeling from the waist down. At the hospital the doctor confirmed that he had broken his back and would spend the rest of his life in a wheelchair. Mark was angry with God. "Why did You do this to me?"

During rehabilitation he met a young Christian who was radiant in spite of her multiple sclerosis. Mark told her he was a Christian too, but he realized that there was a difference. She talked freely about the Lord while he was more interested in the insurance money he would collect.

When Mark was about 32, he reverted to as sinful a lifestyle as his paralysis would allow. But something or Someone led him to attend a church near his house. That was strange, because it was not a Catholic church. What was a nice Catholic fellow like him doing in a Protestant church? The pastor quickly befriended him and began to share the gospel with him. He told Mark that he was a sinner and that he must repent and receive Christ as his Savior from sin. Mark was both offended and puzzled. How did Pastor Jack know so much about him?

All during this time his sister and brother-in-law in Jasper, Alabama, were praying for his salvation. In fact, they met every morning with their employees in their tree trimming business for prayer.

For three or four days Mark experienced deep conviction of sin, even to the point of prolonged weeping. Then came surrender. Thoroughly broken, he acknowledged before God that he was a sinner and asked the Lord to forgive him. Peace came instantly. The war was over.

In the days that followed, God brought a wonderful wife to him, and friends from a Bible Chapel who *"explained to him the way of God more accurately"* (Acts 18:26).

Today Mark accepts his paralysis with submission to the Lord. He says,

I believe that my 35-foot fall was God's intervention in my life. A shepherd sometimes has to break the leg of a wayward sheep to stop it from going astray. The Lord had to break my back to stop me from wandering and to bring me to Himself.

At the time, I was angry with God but I have come to be at peace with my circumstances. This peace has come from the realization that Christ died to save me from sure destruction. When I realized that a price had to be paid to atone for my sins, and that Jesus paid that price for me, my paralysis seemed to be very insignificant. When I could walk and was living in sin, it was hard for God to get my attention. He had to take drastic measures to reach me.

I often think of Matthew 18:8 where Jesus says, "If your hand or foot causes you to sin, cut it off and cast it from you. It is better for you to enter into life lame or maimed, rather than having two hands or two feet to be cast into the everlasting fire." The most important thing is eternal life. The short time we spend here is like the flower of grass when compared to eternity. I thank the Father every day for the gift of God which is eternal life through Jesus Christ our Lord.

CALL THE POLICE

It was a routine call and since everything was quiet on Officer Tom Rodrigues's beat, he decided to take the call, even if it wasn't in his territory. He little realized the eternal consequences that would flow from that casual decision.

He took off in his patrol car for the address the dispatcher had given. There he met Rick and Irene. The stereo tape deck had been stolen from their car. They weren't unduly upset but felt that the police should know about it. Rick had already explained to Irene that he knew something about police work and that stolen property never returns to the owner, so there was no use in sorrowing over it. The best thing to do is forget it.

Tom went to the kitchen to make out the report. He noticed that Irene told the two boys to thank Jesus before they ate their meal, so possibly she was a believer. His hunch was right. But he detected nothing about Rick that made him think he was a Christian—a decent sort of fellow but probably not converted.

As soon as Tom finished the report, he took off to scout out the neighborhood. He knew it well. Soon he saw a young woman who he had reason to believe might be a help. Did she know anyone who might have stolen a tape deck? She suggested that the officer might contact Pancho (not his real name) and gave the address.

A grandmother answered the door. She became extremely agitated when a policeman wanted to see her grandson, but she called Pancho to come to the door. Tom asked him to follow him away from the house so that the grandmother would not become hysterical. By then Pancho's father came from the back yard to see what was going on. Tom explained that he was trying to track down a stolen stereo and had reason to believe that Pancho was involved. He explained his reasons in detail.

At first the suspect denied everything. His father kept saying, "You'd better tell the truth to Officer Rodrigues. I know this officer and you'd better come clean." Finally Pancho broke down and confessed. When the father heard that, he came unglued. "Was that the tape deck you sold to me for $50?" The son admitted that it was. By this time the father was really upset.

Tom wrote out his report, retrieved the stereo, and went back to Rick and Irene's house with it. Within two hours of the officer's first visit, they had their stereo back. As they talked inside the house, Tom said to Rick, "Say, I'll be speaking next Sunday at our church. Would you be interested in coming?"

They did come, and come, and come. A believer named John began meeting with Rick on a weekly basis, going over the gospel in great detail. For a while Rick had difficulty understanding what "being saved" meant. Night after night he would wake up troubled. There was some roadblock but he wasn't sure what it was. There was a gap he couldn't bridge.

Finally he understood. As a Catholic he had been taught that Christ died for the sins of the world. He had always known that. But now it dawned on him, "Christ died for me." As the truth gripped his soul, he realized what he must do. He confessed his sinful condition, that he was not fit for heaven, and that if he received what he deserved he would go to hell. Then by a definite act of faith, he received Jesus Christ as his Lord and Savior. Shortly thereafter he publicly confessed his faith in the waters of believers' baptism. He and Irene were now one in Christ.

God can use even a stolen tape deck as a means of finding a lost sheep. And a witnessing believer like Officer

Tom Rodrigues can reach people that a professional preacher never could. *"How unsearchable are* [God's] *judgments and His ways past finding out"* (Rom. 11:33).

OUT OF CONTROL

Quong Wing was raised in a typical Chinese-American family with parents who did their best to see that he would become a decent, upstanding citizen. Of course, there was always the clash of the two cultures, and Quong Wing elected to go with the flow—that is, the American flow. He did well up until the seventh grade, but then some of his classmates began to bully him relentlessly. He was "a shrimp," was not good in athletics, and seldom made a team in organized sports. To avoid getting beaten up daily, he decided to learn martial arts, but life worsened. He stole, lied, did drugs, and became a violent delinquent. Several times he contemplated suicide.

During his early days of high school, he attended a Chinese Bible Church with his sister and brothers, but that didn't last. Soon he was using drugs daily. Like many of his peers, he found it difficult to submit to authority. Frequent arguments broke out with his parents. He wanted to do his own thing.

His family became less important, and life revolved around his friends. As far as he was concerned, all Chinese fellows were either nerds or hoods (gangsters). He chose the latter. This meant carrying a knife, throwing his weight around, and getting into fights. When he pulled a gun on a vice principal, the police took him home and his father punished him. Life was out of control.

After being expelled from high school when he was a junior, he decided to go to a private school where he had to pay $1,500, money he had been saving to buy a car. Even then he cut classes regularly.

His friends would pick him up each night and they would cruise around looking for trouble. Once, when a car cut them off, they chased it for miles until it entered a dead end street and smashed into a barrier. They slashed the tires of the crashed car and left; the terrified occupants had locked themselves inside the car.

They had frequent scrapes with the law but Quong Wing somehow escaped with nothing more than two hours in the slammer.

In a curious twist of irony, he decided to attend Merritt College and major in Administration of Justice with an option in Law Enforcement. He and his friends drifted apart. He spent five years at Merritt, then transferred to two other universities. The only thing that kept him in college was his interest in the opposite sex. He finally graduated at age 25. Life was empty; suicide was still an option.

A year later he landed a job as a Group Counselor in the county Probation Department. If he thought this would be the answer to his search, he was mistaken. Some of the staff were the scum of society, who had worse problems than the wards. Some were drug addicts, adulterers, womanizers, and suspected child molesters. For three years Quong Wing's main problems were with the staff.

His next position was Deputy Probation Officer, assigned to work with prison parolees who were on probation. From there he was switched to a Juvenile Division camp. No matter where he went, he faced problem after problem. The gears never seemed to mesh. Everything seemed out of kilter. Wasn't there any place where he could find fulfillment? Even his marriage to Cynthia in 1992 didn't bring the peace and satisfaction for which he was searching. Conditions could hardly get worse. But they did.

Quong Wing was transferred to the Intake/In Custody unit at Juvenile Hall and assigned to a supervisor who obviously felt called to make life as intolerable as possible for his staff. Quong Wing had frequent blowouts with him. He so dreaded coming to work that he frequently called in sick. The stress finally erupted as a case of shingles.

The best thing that came out of this firestorm was that a fellow named Dan suggested that Quong Wing seek the real meaning of life. That started him on the search for truth, He studied Zen Buddhism, Taoism, Emotions Anonymous, Psychotherapy, Anger Management—yes, and God's Word. Quong Wing recalls that "the Lord sent tons of believers across my path," but he wasn't ready for them yet. He attended a Bible study at work and went to a huge evangelistic rally in the state capital. The Spirit of God was doing His wonderful work.

His salvation crisis occurred on November 1, 1995. That Sunday in the church he was attending, people were given the opportunity to tell how they came to know the Lord and how He had changed their life. Quong Wing thought he was saved. Because he had made a profession of faith years ago when he attended the Chinese Bible Church, he volunteered to participate in the testimony meeting. Afterwards, two of the Christians came and pointed out that all he had done was tell about the troubles he had. He had never mentioned the name of the Lord. They doubted that he had ever given his heart to Him. One suggested he go home and receive the Lord Jesus Christ as his Lord and Savior.

Alone that night he saw his need of the Savior. He knew he was a sinner and ought to repent. He had determined to look for the truth, and now Christ was presenting Himself to Quong Wing as the way, the truth, and the life. He realized that the Lord Jesus had died on the Cross to pay the penalty of his sins. Without further delay, he made a definite commitment to the Savior. Peace flooded his soul.

Christ makes a difference when He comes into a life.

Quong Wing likes to recount some of the wonderful changes he has experienced. The Lord gave him power to break his addictions without experiencing withdrawal. God brought other sins to his attention so that he could confess and forsake them. When Satan worked overtime to put doubt and fear in his mind, the Lord strengthened him through the Word. He developed a new love for others and a new desire to share Christ with them. His marriage showed a dramatic change for the better. Today Cynthia and he have a baby son.

Quong Wing still is not sinless, of course, but he does sin less. He is not free from temptation, but he has God-sent power to resist it. Life still has problems, but he has Someone to whom to take the problems. He has a new love of holiness and a new hatred of sin. He is leading a Bible study at work and another at a junior high school.

He speaks of himself as a willing and available servant who hopes to continue possessing a teachable heart.

Quong Wing is an example of what God can do with a life that was once out of control.

GINGER'S STORY[10]

Ginger's real name is Virginia Hearn. One of the remarkable features of her spiritual pilgrimage is the number and variety of contacts the Lord used to edge her to faith in Christ. There were churches with a wide spectrum of doctrinal variations. There were Sunday schools, camps, and tent meetings. Parents, personal friends, and books played an important role. It was clear that she was the object of a divine love that would not let her go. Let her tell the story.

> Like so many children, I was taught by my father to say the Lord's prayer every night—but I recall only rattling it off mechanically, as fast as possible, with no thought of what the

words meant, or of talking to a Father in heaven who was listening. I also recall occasionally giving snippy answers to Sunday school teachers, thinking it was funny.

Sunday school was a "given," but unrelated to my family's life beyond the church door. Something gave me a sensitivity to divine names, and I would refuse to sing the words *God* or *Jesus* when they came in the songs. My sister and I without fail earned Sunday school attendance prizes. One prize was a Catholic girl's book. I wondered why the teacher had chosen it, because it was different from our own religion.

A World War I comrade of my father's was "converted" and came to visit us. I had seen such a "conversion" take place in the movie *Sergeant York,* and I knew it meant a changed and good life. My parents were embarrassed by this man's religious fanaticism, but put up with it. He supplied us with strange fundamentalist books and papers, which I read without conviction. I was indifferent to the points they were trying to make.

One of the mystifying experiences of my childhood was that we went to some summer tent meetings held by itinerant evangelists. They were loud and strange. Some people cried and "went forward," but not my parents. At the encouragement of a family friend, we went to special meetings at the Assembly of God church in town. Some people wanted to be healed, but weren't.

During the summer there was daily vacation Bible school held at a "stricter" church in our neighborhood, and no one had to force me to go. I learned all the books of the Bible, and there was a long poem giving a "summary" of the contents of its 66 books:

In Genesis the world was made by God's creative hand;
In Exodus the Hebrews marched to reach the Promised
Land...

> The Revelation prophesies of that tremendous day,
> When Christ, and Christ alone, shall be the trembling
>   sinner's stay.

I learned songs and games and maps of Bible lands and probably some Bible verses—and excelled in my teacher's eyes—but in my heart I was personally untouched by it all. On our eighth birthday my mother had given us a Bible with our names in gold letters and showed us the Twenty-third Psalm. I revered the Bible but did not read it.

My personal arrival at the "age of accountability" had been a clear event to me. We were having a second-grade spelling test and *field* was one of the words. Try as I would, I couldn't remember if it was *ie* or *ei*. So I wrote the correct spelling on the desk for ready reference when the test came. I knew that was wrong—yet I did it.

Over the years the knowledge of my own lostness grew, though I wouldn't have described it that way. At age 13, I was "confirmed." Together we all recited a confirmation covenant that said:

> Lord Jesus, take this heart of mine,
> Make it pure and wholly Thine.
> Thou wast born and died for me.
> I will henceforth live for Thee.

The long weeks of Saturday morning confirmation classes in our liberal church hadn't explained religious things along those lines at all. I sensed the discrepancy, but didn't care enough to question it. Yet that confirmation morning, I meant what I said, and I hoped it would make a difference.

The summer after eighth grade I went to a Methodist church camp with a friend. There I heard about Christian "missions" in foreign lands and met some real-life missionaries. At the end of the camp each person was asked to write a letter about what that week at camp had meant. The letter would be mailed back to each one a few months later. I had gained a sense for God that week and vowed to live for Him. Then I went back home and the inspiration ended. When my letter came, shortly before Christmas, I tore it up without reading it. I was ashamed of whatever emotion had been conjured up the past summer, and I knew that nothing had come of it.

In junior high science, we read how various cosmic events involving flaming balls and tremendous gravitational forces had resulted in our solar system and this life on this planet had developed. Nothing was said about God. When one spunky little girl made a big fuss about God's being left out, the teacher tried to explain it somehow, but he was embarrassed and she was unrelenting.

Until my senior year, high school was a spiritually barren time. One girl in my class was a Christian, and I admired her. She was different—quiet and serene, an excellent but noncompetitive student—who attended that "stricter" church. Although I once asked her about her religion, she wasn't able to articulate her faith in the high school milieu. In a theme for my American Problems class, I wrote about the need for people to have faith in some great Power, of man's incompleteness and failure, of the ideal of dedicating one's life to God. It was a spiritual breakthrough—away from sole interest in *me* and whatever acquisitions I could make or honors I could win. In college I started to read the Bible my mother had given me 10 years before, but I didn't understand it. I began dating a fellow who had some kind of Christian faith, but his religion sounded childish to me. After some months I recognized that my goals in life were different from his, and I cruelly broke up with him.

The next year I made a close friend, Joy, at the beginning of the school year. She was part of a religious group called an "assembly." She cared for me and spent time with me. She wanted my friendship. Further, she invited me to a "study" she and another girl were having in our dorm. I went because of our friendship. And in that study, the gospel dawned on me as "good news." We were reading from Newell's commentary on Romans, *Some Words About Grace.*[9]

> Grace is uncaused in the recipient…There being no cause in the creature why Grace should be shown, the creature must be brought off from trying to give cause to God for His grace.
>
> Man has been accepted in Christ…
>
> He is not "on probation."

Through those words, I grasped what I hadn't grasped before. That for failure there is forgiveness and cleansing. That in one's weakness Christ's strength can be found. That God is a present help in trouble. I began to read the Bible earnestly for the first time, surprised now to understand what it said.

Three weeks later, I went home for Thanksgiving. My youngest sister, then a high school senior, had gotten into a teenage Bible discussion group in another church in our town, and had come to personal faith in Christ.

"Listen," I said to my other sister, then a college freshman, "you've got to start reading the Bible for yourself." In coming months the gospel touched her as well, and the three of us found new unity in our common Christian faith.

A CABLE OR JESUS

In 1991 Ian visited an older cousin in California. Although brought up in a godly home, he was not a decided Christian.

His cousin felt sure that Ian would like to visit Yosemite

National Park and climb Half Dome, so he asked two young believers (we'll call them Eric and Dan) if they would like to go and make the climb with Ian. The foursome reserved a housekeeping cabin on the floor of the valley and took a supply of food.

On the appointed day they had an early breakfast, then the three young fellows started out. The cousin's job was to read and study during the day, then have supper ready for them when they returned that night.

The last part of the climb is over smooth granite, curved like the top half of a ball. It is impossible to walk in an upright position. A climber must pull himself up between two cables, holding on for dear life. It is best not to look back.

The three fellows reached the top safely, enjoyed their brown bag lunch, marveled at the grand vista for a while, and then started down. Once again a firm grip on the cables was necessary for survival.

Eric was first, Dan was second, then Ian. A total stranger was pulling himself up on the cables while they were descending. He passed Eric, then passed Dan, but when he got to Ian, he asked, "Are you trusting that cable or are you trusting Jesus?" It was a bolt out of the blue, or, as the Bible says, a bow at a venture. Ian said that he was trusting Jesus to hold the cable.

Later, when the cousin heard about this incident, he thought to himself, "I think the Lord is chasing you, Ian, and I don't think you'll get away."

When Ian returned home, life seemed emptier than before. He sensed that his life was lacking direction and purpose. There was a deep conviction that he had to do something to change his lifestyle. However, this compulsion to change gradually waned and he went back to his old ways. The load of guilt was mounting.

In 1996 he felt desperate enough to attend an evangelical church. Three things impressed him there. The people made him feel welcome. The Holy Spirit was obviously present. The preaching was true to the Bible.

When he watched the Christians participating in the communion service, he had great feelings of guilt and sorrow. The guilt was conviction of sin, and the sorrow was knowing that salvation was free for the taking but he was not willing to accept it.

Finally, on November 16, 1997, he confessed his many sins to the Lord, acknowledged his inability to save himself, and asked for forgiveness and for God's saving grace. He put his trust in the Lord. Ian publicly confessed Christ as his Lord and Savior that day.

So, has life changed? Ian is no longer reticent in talking about the Lord. He has a new hunger to study the Word. He has a new joy in seeing others come to Christ. And his life no longer lacks direction and purpose.

CONCLUSION

The wonders of God in creation exceed our powers of tabulation or comprehension. The universe He spoke into being is greater than any of us can know. It defies dimension. We stand amazed at the number of the stars, their magnitude, and precision.

Everything about our planet makes it just right to sustain life. A kindly Providence accurately designed its distance from the sun and moon, its atmosphere, an abundant supply of water, its axis of rotation, and hundreds of other conditions that make it habitable. It is finely tuned.

God's masterpiece is the human body. The cell alone is a world of wonders. Trillions of them go about their business of forming the brain, vital organs, skin, bones, joints, ligaments, muscles, blood, and other necessary componants. And nothing is haphazard. Everything must happen in the proper sequence. The body is all the more remarkable when we realize that the finished product is about 65% water.

Think of the libraries devoted to the study of animals, birds, fish, reptiles, insects, and bacteria. Frankly we haven't scratched the surface in discovering hidden marvels. And that is true of the world's vegetation, essential among other things for food and oxygen, and beauty to enjoy.

The Creator is the God of providence. He supplies the desire of every living (Ps. 145:16). He harnesses circumstances to accomplish His will, and works all things together for good to those who love Him. Our Lord answers prayer according to infinite wisdom, love and power. We see Him in designed coincidences, the marvelous converging of circumstances, and events that would never happen according to the laws of chance or probability.

Our wonderful God is also the Redeemer, saving and transforming human rejects and self-righteous Pharisees. It is He who loves the unlovely and redeems the unlikely. In wonderful grace He populates heaven with people who deserve the opposite. Only Jesus can give beauty for ashes, the oil of joy for mourning, and the garment of praise for the spirit of heaviness (Isa. 61:3). In Him the restless find rest, the blind see, and slaves find freedom.

But the greatest of all wonders is this: the Creator and Sustainer of the universe is the same One who died on the Cross of Calvary. In infinite love, He took the sinner's place and died to pay the penalty of the condemned. Nothing can ever surpass the marvel of this: "Christ, the mighty Maker, died for man His creature's sin" (Isaac Watts).

 ENDNOTES

PART I

1 J. P. Moreland, ed., *The Creation Hypothesis,* Downers Grove, IL: InterVarsity Press, 1994, p. 164.

2 Ibid.

3 Ibid.

4 Ibid.

5 A. Naismith, *1200 More Notes, Quotes, and Anecdotes,* London: Pickering and Inglis Ltd., 1975, p. 225.

6 *Nature's Masterpieces*, Reader's Digest Assn. Ltd., 1997, p. 6.

7 Quoted in "Jesus and the Big Bang," Philip Yancey, *Christianity Today*, July 14, 1997, p. 80.

8 Lewis Thomas, *The Medusa and the Snail*, New York: The Viking Press, 1979, p. 199.

9 The Reader's Digest Assn., 1969, pp. 26, 28.
10 Washington, D.C.: National Geographic Society, 1986, p. 7.

11 *Thinking About the Brain*, IMPACT #200, Institute for Christian Research, El Cajon, CA, p. 4.

12 *Time* magazine, April 6, 1998, p. 75.

13 Don Hillis, *Does God Have Gray Hair?* Self-published, p. 8.

14 Dr. Paul Brand and Philip Yancey, *In His Image,* Grand Rapids, MI: Zondervan, 1987, p. 129.

15 Ibid., p. 110.

16 F. B. Meyer, *Joseph—Beloved, Hated, Exalted.* Fort Washington, PA: Christian Literature Crusade, 1060, p. 73.

17 Lewis Thomas, *Lives of a Cell*, New York: The Viking Press, 1974, p. 66.

18 *The Incredible Machine*, National Geographic Society, p. 13.

19 Quoted in *Our Daily Bread*, August 5, 1997, Grand Rapids, MI: Radio Bible Class.

20 *Smithsonian,* April 1996, pp. 92-102.

21 *National Geographic,* August 1995, p. 37.

22 *National Geographic*, April 1994, *Jaws of Life.*

23 *Our Daily Bread,* July 8, 1999, Grand Rapids, MI: Radio Bible Class.

24 *National Geographic,* September 1997, p. 141.

25 *National Geographic,* July 1997, Earth Almanac.

26 *Reader's Digest,* August 4, 1966, p. 182.

27 Gary Parker*, Creation: Facts of Life,* Green Forest, AR: Master Books, 1994, pp. 57-58.

28 Adapted from *National Geographic*, "New Spin on Fast Food," quoted in *Our Daily Bread,* November 4, 1998.

29 *National Geographic*, November 1994, Geographica.

30 *Smithsonian,* April 1997, pp. 74-85.

31 Adapted from "For Leaf Cutter Ants, Farm Life Isn't So Simple" by Nicholas Wade, *The New York Times,* August 3, 1999, pp. D1, D4.

32 *The Economist, "Blue Morpho and Magnificent Owl,"* April 5, 1997, p. 80.

33 For background material the author is indebted to Alice Gilbreath, *Antlers and Radar*, New York: David McKay Company, 1978.

34 For helpful research the author is indebted to William Rodriguez.

35 Mark Looy, ICR., IMPACT # 208, p. 1.

36 Quoted in *Reader's Digest*, December 1996, p. 37.

37 Michael Denton, *Evolution: A Theory in Crisis,* Bethesda, MD: Adler and Adler, 1986, p. 77.

38 Michael Behe, *Darwin's Black Box,* New York: #3 Free Press, 1996.

39 Hoyle on Evolution, *Nature* 294, November 12, 1981, p.105.

40 Francis Crick, *Life Itself: Its Origin and Nature,* New York: Simon and Schuster, 1981, p. 88.

41 Carl Sagan, F. H. C. Crick, L. M. Mulkhin, "Extra-terrestrial Life," in *Communication with Extraterrestrial Intelligence (CETI),* Carl Sagan. ed. Cambridge, MA: MIT Press, 1973, pp. 45-46.

42 Quoted in *The Creation Hypothesis,* p. 274.

43 Richard Dawkins, *The Blind Watchmaker,* New York: Norton, 1987, p. 1.

44 Quoted in *Mere Creation*, William A. Dembski, ed., Downers Grove, IL. InterVarsity Press, 1998, p. 237.

45 Ibid. *p.* 30.

PART II

1 The author expresses sincere thanks to the following for providing background information for the articles indicated:

> David Long *Talk About Car Troubles*
> Dena Speering *The Gummed-Up Carburetor*
> Ben Iler *Every Need Supplied*
> Lois Reichle *Warned to Withdraw*
> Milton and Evelyn Johnson *Just the Right Word*
> Sam Mattix *The Treasured New Testament*
> Archie and Virginia Ross *The Black Mamba*
> Charles Shorten *Lost Contact*
> Julie Griffith *The Angel Dog*
> Dick, Betty, and Brad Sanders *My Friend, Brad*

2 Alexander Carson, *The History of Providence,* Grand Rapids, MI: Baker Book House, 1977, pp. 90-91.

3 Adapted from a letter written by Lois Stephen in *Echoes Quarterly Review,* April-June 1977, pp. 28-29.

4 Adapted from *First We Have Coffee* by Margaret Jensen, Eugene, OR: Harvest House Publishers, 1995, pp. 45-53.

5 Ibid., pp. 67-68.

6 Taken from *Open Doors News Brief,* August 1991, p. 8.

7 Condensed from *Ripening Fruit in Southeast Peru by Peggy Covert* in *Missions* magazine, November 1977, pp. 3-7.

8 Adapted from *Voyage to Faith,* Thomas Fleming, *Guideposts*, March 1995, pp. 3-7.

9 Helen Roseveare, *Living Faith*, Minneapolis, MN: Bethany House Publishers, 1980, pp. 44-45. Used by permission.

10 Adapted from "The Providential Escape" by Susan Osborn, *Power*

for Living Magazine, March 3, 1996, as told by Ravi Zacharias, tape #152 *Who Are You God?* Ravi Zacharias, Used by permission of Susan Osborn and Ravi Zacharias International Ministries.

PART III

1 The author expresses sincere thanks to the following for providing background material for the articles indicated:

> Milton Haack *Saved and Sure of It*
> Michael Alonso *The Bible Page with Only Two Words*
> Archie and Virginia Ross *Piliaski*
> Billy Stevenson *O God, Save My Daddy*
> Mark Pease *Mark Pease Finds Peace*
> Tom Rodrigues *Call the Police*
> Mark Soohoo *Out of Control*
> Ian MacLeod *A Cable or Jesus?*

2 Adapted from *God's Wonderful Kindness,* James R. Cochrane in *Missions* magazine, April 1997, pp. 3-5.

3 Not his real name.

4 Adapted from *Encyclopedia Britannica* and a tape titled *The Angelic Devil: Balaam,* by Ravi Zacharias. Source of long quote no longer available.

5 Partly adapted from Letters to the Editor, Sebring, Florida newspaper, March 15, 1998.

6 Tex Watson as told to Chaplain Ray, *Will You Die For Me?* Grand Rapids, MI: Fleming H. Revell Company, a division of Baker Book House Company, 1978, pp. 198-99. Used by permission.

7 Adapted from *Bis zum Ende des Regenbogen (To the End of the Rainbow) in Ruhe der Rastlosen (Rest of the Restless)*, Bielefeld, Germany: CLV, 1990, pp. 7-50.

8 Ruth A. Tucker, *From Jerusalem to Irian Jaya,* Grand Rapids, MI: Academic Books, 1983, pp. 121-131. Adapted from tape #111 *"Is There Not a Cause?"* by Ravi Zacharias. RZIM, 4725 Peachtree Corners Circle, Suite 250, Norcross, GA 30092. Used by permission.

9 Excerpted from a much longer chapter in *What They Did Right: Reflections on Parents by Their Children* by Virginia Hearn, ed., Wheaton, IL: Tyndale House Publishers, 1974, pp. 282-91. Used by permission of the author.

10 *Romans Verse by Verse,* by William R. Newell, Chicago: Moody Press, 1938, pp. 243-247.